D1466985

SEVEN SKIRTS FOR SEVEN SISTERS

REAL-LIFE LESSONS ON PRAYER AND LISTENING TO GOD

"You make known to me the path of life; in your presence there is fullness of joy; at your right hand are pleasures forevermore." Ps. 16:11

DONNA COPPERSMITH

Precious Dolores,

What an awesome joy it was to hear from you & to know that the Lord is still using you as you speak of Him & His presence in your life! I'll always remember your passionate love for Jesus and your devotion to prayer. You were an inspiration to me! Thanks for being such a great model of prayer ~ certainly the LORD has used you to be a light for Him! I can't wait to hear what you think about what the Lord did in my journey! To GOD be the glory! Love & blessings,

Donna

INFINITY
PUBLISHING

All rights reserved. No part of this book shall be reproduced or transmitted in any form or by any means, electronic, mechanical, magnetic, photographic including photocopying, recording or by any information storage and retrieval system, without prior written permission of the publisher. No patent liability is assumed with respect to the use of the information contained herein. Although every precaution has been taken in the preparation of this book, the publisher and author assume no responsibility for errors or omissions. Neither is any liability assumed for damages resulting from the use of the information contained herein.

Copyright © 2017 by Donna Coppersmith

ISBN 978-1-4958-1224-8
ISBN 978-1-4958-1225-5 eBook
Library of Congress Control Number: 2017903208

All Scripture quotations, unless otherwise indicated, are taken from the Holy Bible, New International Version®, NIV®. Copyright ©1973, 1978, 1984, 2011 by Biblica, Inc.™ Used by permission of Zondervan. All rights reserved worldwide. www.zondervan.com The "NIV" and "New International Version" are trademarks registered in the United States Patent and Trademark Office by Biblica, Inc.™

Cover art and design by LaVel Rude.

Published January 2017

INFINITY PUBLISHING
1094 New DeHaven Street, Suite 100
West Conshohocken, PA 19428-2713
Toll-free (877) BUY BOOK
Local Phone (610) 941-9999
Fax (610) 941-9959
Info@buybooksontheweb.com
www.buybooksontheweb.com

DEDICATION

*To my late mother, Edna Mae Hopper Wagner,
a strong and faithful woman of prayer, who not only talked
about praying and listening to God, but lived her life
doing it and giving me a wonderful legacy to pass on.*

*To my daughter, Kristin Noel Bennecker,
a miraculous gift of God in response to the prayers of many. She's
the one who, as a young teenager, literally turned half of her clothes
closet into a "prayer closet," learning early on the absolute necessity of
leaning on God in prayer. Today, she serves Jesus as an advocate for
the poor, the lost and the voiceless, as she boldly demonstrates a life of
praying, listening, and responding to God in her day and generation.*

*To the generations to follow,
that they might "Seek the LORD while he may be found; call on him
while he is near." (Isaiah 55:6)*

CONTENTS

INTRODUCTION

Do you long to grow more fully in a life of praying, listening, and responding to God? If so, *Seven Skirts for Seven Sisters* has been written with you in mind. I believe there is a desperate need for people today to live in deeper intimacy with God, to talk with Him in prayer, listen to Him as He speaks to us, and then to respond to Him in faith-filled expectation and obedience.

Experiencing this in your daily life isn't just wishful thinking. It can really happen by the grace of God and the power of the Holy Spirit. It is my prayer that these true stories you read in *Seven Skirts for Seven Sisters* will inspire you to pursue this kind of life-changing intimacy with God.

This book has been written in such a way that it can be read privately or be used in a small group Bible Study. Either way, I hope you will take advantage of the Reflection Pages at the end of each chapter—by reading the Scriptures, answering the Questions for Reflection and Discussion, and then praying the Reflection Prayer before you go on to the next chapter.

If you use this book in a small group Bible Study, I recommend that the participants cover one chapter per session. Prior to each session, participants could read the chapter on their own and prayerfully reflect on the Scriptures and Questions at the end of each chapter. When the small group meets, you might find the following agenda helpful:

1. Open with prayer.
2. Read aloud the Scriptures at the end of the chapter.

3. Discuss your answers to the Questions.

4. Share any additional personal prayer needs.

5. Pray together as a group.

6. Close by praying aloud together the Prayer at the end of the chapter.

Writing *Seven Skirts for Seven Sisters* has been an adventure of grace for me. I would like to thank my family and friends who have encouraged me, and prayed for me, in my writing journey. I'm grateful to all the women who gave and received the skirts mentioned in this book. Of each of them, it can be said: *"She is clothed with strength and dignity, she can laugh at the days to come. She speaks with wisdom, and faithful instruction is on her tongue." (Proverbs 31:25–26).* I'm thankful to my friend of many decades, LaVel Rude, who lovingly painted the picture that graces the cover of this book. I also want to express my love and thanks to my husband, Mike, my best friend and partner in life and ministry. He's the one who not only encouraged me to write this book, but also came alongside of me with his continual help and support—going through the writing process together drew us even closer to the Lord and each other. And finally, I give thanks to my Savior, Jesus, who made me His own and has graciously done so much in my life. To Him goes all the glory!

"Let us then approach the throne of grace with confidence, so that we may receive mercy and find grace to help us in our time of need." (Hebrews 4:16)

Donna Coppersmith
Georgetown, Texas

CHAPTER ONE

THE GATHERING OF THE SKIRTS

I sat on my bed surrounded by dozens of skirts. The skirts had all kinds of different designs—some skirts were dressy, some were casual. Some skirts were complete outfits with a vest or a jacket. Some were long and flowing, while others were shorter and fitted. They were many different colors—some were bright, and others subdued. And they were different sizes—some were smaller, others larger. Like some women, I was accustomed to going shopping, coming home with outfits, laying them out on my bed, and then trying them on—even modeling them to my husband. But I wouldn't be doing any of that with these skirts. God had showed me that I wouldn't be keeping any of them. Instead, I'd be giving every one of them away; not to women I already knew, but to women I would soon meet. In less than twenty-four hours, I would be on a plane to Africa, and I was taking these skirts with me. As I carefully and prayerfully folded each skirt and put it in a suitcase, my mind drifted back to when I was a child in the 1950s....

Life was so much different back then. On Sundays, most businesses, retail stores, and even gas stations were closed in my hometown of Abilene, Texas. People actually set aside time in their schedules to go to church and Sunday school. Every Sunday, my father and brother got dressed in their suit coats and ties. My mom made sure my two sisters and I wore our "Sunday best" shoes, which had been polished the day before. We also donned dresses that Mom had sewn for us. These dresses were usually made from feed sacks, the patterns of which we got to pick out from the stacks of bags at the feed store. Even though our white wooden church with its small steeple was old, it was usually packed on Sunday mornings. This little church was an important part of my childhood years.

One of the highlights of my early memories at our church occurred at the annual Missionary Sunday. This was a time when missionaries and their families came from all over the world to tell their stories. Several hours after our morning worship service, women brought big bowls of food and placed them on long tables set up on the lawn outside the church. After eating way too much yummy, melt-in-your mouth Texas barbecue that had been cooking all day, we kids stood in long lines for little cone-shaped cups of a cherry-red flavored drink, which was a real treat in those days. When cold watermelon was pulled out of the ice-filled aluminum washtubs and cut into slices, we ate bites of it and then went running around the churchyard, spitting seeds at one another. It was great fun! Life was surely good when we were handed a little cup of vanilla ice cream—something most of us rarely had the opportunity to enjoy back then.

The main event of the day came when the steeple bells rang out, signaling everyone to assemble inside the unair-conditioned church. The ceiling fans spun on high speed to move the stale warm air, and the arch-shaped windows were opened all the way to the top, hopefully to catch an evening breeze. A slide projector was set up on the red-carpeted aisle, and a big white screen loomed shakily right up in front. The missionaries stood, shared their stories, and showed their pictures. Then the organist would begin playing from the balcony. Sitting on the hard oak pews, we all loudly sang out what eventually became familiar, even memorized, hymns.

One year, when I was around ten years old, missionaries came from Africa. I was strangely alert as they shared their stories. And when the organist played the song, *"'Hark!' the Voice of Jesus Crying,"* something inside of me stirred as the congregation sang the words:

"Hark!" the voice of Jesus crying, "Who will go and work today? Fields are white and harvests waiting, Who will bear the sheaves away?"

Loud and long the Master calleth, Rich reward He offers thee;

Who will answer, gladly saying, "Hear am I, send me, send me!"

I fought back tears that were welling up from inside of me. These feelings were definitely new to me. Overwhelmed and embarrassed, I didn't understand what was happening. While wiping tears away, on the inside I truly felt like jumping up and saying, *"I'll go! I'll go!"* I can only describe it as a deep yearning, which I now know to be a *"call."* I later learned I was experiencing the presence of God in a brand-new way.

Sitting there in that little church in Abilene, Texas, I began to think, and daydream, about going to Africa. It seemed like an impossible dream. How could a little girl like me, growing up in a lower-middle class family, ever get to faraway Africa? I didn't know it at the time, but now I know it was the Holy Spirit planting seeds in my heart, preparing me for what was to come.

In the years that followed, I saw God work in my life in many ways. I married a wonderful pastor—my husband, Mike—and we served in several churches in Northern Minnesota, followed by thirty-one years of ministry in Palm Springs, California. During those years, I had a long teaching career in both Christian and public schools.

My husband and I went through several miscarriages as well as the death of our infant son, Adam. Then we had the privilege of raising an awesome daughter, Kristin. I even had the opportunity to travel to, and teach in, several countries on short-term mission trips. But, curiously, I still had that yearning deep inside of me to go to Africa. And every time I'd hear an invitation from a speaker asking, "Who will go into the world?" in my heart I would say, *"Here am I! I'll go. Send me!"*

In the summer of 2005, our daughter Kristin had finished her first year of college. Sensing she was being called to go on a missions trip, she prayed. Doors opened for her to spend two months in several countries in Africa. I truly felt like she was carrying forth the dream God had been planted in my heart way back when I was a ten-year-old child. Upon her return, it was exhilarating for me to see the impact the trip had on her and how the Holy Spirit had used her so significantly. She now had a passionate commitment, a calling, to be a full-time missionary serving Christ among the poor, lost, and needy people of this world.

A family photo with Kristin before she headed off to her second year of college.

At the end of the summer, not long after Kristin had gone back to college, I walked out of our Sunday morning worship service in Palm Springs and began to greet people. Barbara, a longtime member of the church, rushed up to me. She was aglow with excitement, and I knew immediately something unusual had happened. Words of joy tumbled out of her mouth as she exclaimed, "I'm going to Africa!" She went on to explain that she had been asked to speak at a number of conferences, orphanages, prisons, and refugee camps in several African countries. She would be gone for nearly four weeks. Without any hesitation, I asked, "Who is going with you to be your prayer support?" She stepped backwards with a wide-eyed look and immediately responded, "I think you are." Instantly, we both sensed a presence we knew to be the Holy Spirit. It was a breathtaking moment. Right there, in the courtyard of our church, we prayed together that the Lord would lead us and make it clear to us if this was to happen. We agreed to take the time for each of us to continue to pray and wait on the Lord. So that's exactly what we did. We prayed and prayed, read His Word, and waited. I asked the Lord to speak to me and give me confirmation as to whether or not I was to go with Barbara to Africa.

I also asked my husband, my family, and others to pray about it. I was concerned about the financial costs of the trip; but every time I thought about the costs, it seemed like the Lord would impress my mind with the words, Don't worry about that. In addition, because I was working, I needed to get a month-long leave of absence from my part-time job as a homeschool consultant. When I asked my boss, she readily concurred, giving me permission and saying, "You go, girl!" Everywhere I turned, I saw AFRICA. The Lord allowed me to see scenes from Africa on television and reports about Africa on the internet, as well as in newspapers and magazines.

After several days of this, the confirming word I had asked from God finally came to me. As I was reading my Bible, the Lord led me to a verse in the Old Testament. I had read this verse before, but now it spoke to me in a new way. *"Have I not commanded you? Be strong and courageous. Do not be terrified; do not be discouraged, for the LORD your God will be with you wherever you go."* (Joshua 1:9) I read and reread these words of Joshua 1:9. I prayed over them many times throughout the next few days. Every time I prayed, I sensed God's Spirit repeatedly saying these words to me: *GO! You are able. You will have all that you need when you need it. Don't worry about the finances. Nothing is too difficult for Me. Step out! Trust Me. Don't forget. Remember how I helped you in the past.* The Lord was already giving me words that I would later need, and would return to often, during my time in Africa.

So I had my answer. In a childlike way, I literally jumped up and down, running around the large island in our kitchen and shouting, "Yippee! I am going to Africa!" In the next moment, my thoughts warped back to that little church in Texas when I was a young girl. It was as though something suddenly erupted inside of me—the childhood dream I had when we were singing the words of that old hymn, "*Who will answer gladly saying, 'Here am I, send me, send me!'?*" Those seeds that had been planted in my heart were bursting out of me! That dream was turning into a reality!

After talking with my husband, I excitedly called Barbara to tell her the decision the Lord had given me. She said she knew, even before I called, that I'd be going. For both of us, this was a confirmation from the Lord that He was bringing everything together as we waited on Him. The time we had spent in seeking God, and also having others pray for His Spirit's leading, was an important step in preparing us for what would be coming our way in Africa. We were learning just how faithful the Lord is to all those who will not just rush ahead, but also will call upon His name and then wait on Him. He was teaching us to not leave out this part out of our decision-making process, but to wait upon Him!

In the days that followed, I started seeing God honor the words He had given to me. Barbara told me she was impressed by the Lord to pay for all my airline tickets. I would need to cover other expenses on my own. And soon other people came along, wanting to help me with these expenses. Surely God was at work to get me to Africa! It gave me great peace to know that the Lord was attentive to my every need.

Needless to say, the next few weeks were highly intense ones. There was much to be done! I was busy working at my job and finishing up projects before I was to leave. Not only was I packing my bags, but I was also preparing and freezing meals for my dear husband to have when I'd be gone. I had to get my passport in order, and get all the required shots I would need to travel abroad. In addition to all of this, I was constantly on the hunt asking the Lord to lead me as I gathered little things to take to the children in orphanages, purchased personal hygiene items and school supplies, and picked up many donated Bibles to be given to people in the hospitals, prisons, and refugee camps. Since my purpose in going to Africa was to be praying for Barbara, I knew I had to take time to pray and read God's Word each day as part of these preparations for our trip.

Then something happened. Less than a week before our departure, Barbara and I received a phone call from a newly married couple who had organized the trip and with whom we'd be traveling. In this book, I'll call them Bob and Kathy. This would be Kathy's seventh time to travel to Africa. They were in the process of gathering many donated items from folks around their area. Knowing the circumstances of many of the African people they'd met from previous trips, they already knew what things were needed. They planned to take these items in large plastic containers, and would distribute them as the Lord directed during our time in Africa. Bob and Kathy had a special request for us: they wanted Barbara and me to each bring thirty long skirts. We were to wear one of these skirts each day and then give the skirt away to an African woman. We were stunned. How in the world would we possibly have the time or the finances to pull all that together in only a few days?

Feeling desperate and overwhelmed, I cried out to the Lord, *"How can I ever do all this?"* Then I heard it—a now-familiar inner voice saying, *Did I not say to you that you would have all that you need when you need it?* Almost instantaneously, a thought came to me to call my sisters, Jan and Sharon. They lived about three hundred miles away. A few weeks prior, they had both informed me they believed the Lord had told them they were to do everything they could to help me go on this trip. I picked up the phone and called them, telling them of my need for thirty long skirts. Without hesitation, they replied, "Don't worry. We've got this!" They both went to work, prayerfully gathering up the skirts I needed.

Exactly one day before Barbara and I left for the airport to fly to Africa, a box arrived from my sisters. Inside were a number of things that friends of Jan and Sharon had sent for us to give away on our journey in Africa. But, most importantly, inside this box were thirty worn skirts. My first thought was, *Oh, no! These aren't new skirts!* Then I discovered that my sisters had invited ladies in the their church to prayerfully choose, from their own closets, a gently worn skirt that would be given to a woman in Africa. These women prayed and then graciously pulled out of their closets just the right skirt. Pinned inside each one of those precious skirts was a note with the name of the woman who had given the skirt. Also written on each one of the notes was the woman's profession, along with her God-given gift or role in serving Jesus. I was blessed that my sisters had thoughtfully pinned the notes inside each skirt. Not only that, they took time and prayed over each one of the skirts and all the other items that had been gathered for God's purposes in Africa. Through their ongoing prayers and gifts, my dear sisters and their friends were investing part of themselves in my journey. These gifts would multiply the joy of what was to come—not only for those who would receive them, but also for those who gave them!

Now I sat on my bed with the skirts all around me. Picking one up and holding it in my hands, I knew that I could not just haphazardly give away a skirt each day. I wanted God's blessing to be connected to every single one of these skirts. Because the skirts had been lovingly chosen through prayer, I needed to do the same thing with them. Where and to whom should I give a skirt? Which skirt would I choose and why? I knew without a doubt that I first needed to pray and then wait for the Lord to impress me with some sort of direction for each skirt. And, in the weeks to follow, the Lord did just that! Each skirt would become a "God Story" of His unfailing love and His powerful work in people's lives.

As you read this, you might be tempted to ask: "Can God really use a worn skirt to teach a lesson? I know He spoke through lilies of the field, a loaf of bread, and even a donkey. But a skirt?" The answer to this question is "Yes!" In this book, you are going to read seven stories of some of the many skirts that I gave away during the weeks that I was in Africa. In each one of these seven skirt stories, you will meet a wonderful Christian "sister" who received one or more of these skirts. It is my prayer that each skirt story will unfold to you a powerful lesson on *how to pray, listen, and respond to God.*

Preparing to depart for Africa, I put these skirts in a suitcase and closed the lid. How God was going to use them would be revealed to me in the days ahead. But, for now, Barbara and I were all packed, giddy with anticipation, and filled with excitement. We were ready to see our dreams unfold. Here I was, all grown up, but still feeling on the inside like that ten-year-old girl from a town in Texas who had heard the voice of Jesus calling. Now, by His grace and in His time, I was going! Remembering the words that the Holy Spirit had stirred in my heart so many years before, I prayed, *"Here am I! Send me. Send me!"* It was happening! I was on my way!

CHAPTER ONE - REFLECTION PAGES
"If you want to pray, listen, and respond to God...."

PRAY AND LISTEN TO GOD AS YOU READ THESE WORDS FROM THE BIBLE

Job 33:14
For God does speak—now one way, now another—though man may not perceive it.

John 10:3b–4
He calls his own sheep by name and leads them out. When he has brought out all his own, he goes on ahead of them, and his sheep follow him because they know his voice.

1 Samuel 3:10
The LORD came and stood there, calling as at the other times, "Samuel! Samuel!" Then Samuel said, "Speak, for your servant is listening."

2 Chronicles 16:9a
For the eyes of the LORD range throughout the earth to strengthen those whose hearts are fully committed to him.

Jeremiah 29:11-14a
"For I know the plans I have for you," declares the LORD, "plans to prosper you and not to harm you, plans to give you a hope and a future. Then you will call upon me and come and pray to me, and I will listen to you. You will seek me and find me when you seek me with all your heart. I will be found by you...."

Psalm 138:8
The LORD will fulfill his purpose for me; your love, O LORD, endures forever—do not abandon the works of your hand.

John 15:7
If you remain in me, and my words remain in you, ask whatever you wish, and it will be given to you.

QUESTIONS FOR REFLECTION AND DISCUSSION

1. What was one thing that particularly spoke to you in this first chapter? Describe what you think God was saying to you through it.

2. In what ways do you believe God is still speaking to His people today?

3. What do you struggle with when it comes to praying, listening, and responding to God?

4. Read about the call of Isaiah the prophet in Isaiah 6:1–8 in your Bible. What do these verses have to say about praying, listening, and responding to God?

5. Have you ever had a time when God gave you a "dream" or you felt that God had called you to do something? If so, describe what it was.

6. Have you abandoned that dream, and if so, how did that happen? Do you want to pursue that dream, and if so, how can you do that?

7. What is one thing you are going to be praying about as a result of your time in this chapter?

PRAYER OF RESPONSE

Lord Jesus, fill me with a renewed passion to know You and love You with all my heart, just as You have loved me so completely. Give me an open mind and a hungering heart to hear from You through the many ways You want to speak to me. Thank You for Your Word which leads the way—help me to read the Scriptures with fresh eyes of faith. I trust that You have specific plans and purposes for my life, and that You will fulfill these in me. As I read these skirt stories, reignite within me a greater understanding of my past, a clearer perspective of my present, and a greater hope for my future. Grow Your "dream" in my heart! Help me to take time to listen for Your voice. Develop within me a longing to talk with You and not at You. Use Your Word and these stories to accomplish Your will for me. And thank You that You will be with me, giving me all I need to step out in faith and to have the courage to follow You. In Your loving name I pray. Amen!

CHAPTER TWO

THE FIRST SKIRT STORY— VIOLET

If you want to pray, listen, and respond to God…
In the face of fear, call upon God right away and be willing to
act upon His Word, not your fears.

I t was around midnight when the crackling sound of the intercom woke us. The pilot announced that our plane was beginning its slow descent to the airport in Nairobi, Kenya. Barbara pushed up the window shade and we wiped sleep out of our eyes as we peered into the dark sky, looking for the skyline of Nairobi—a city that then housed almost a million people. Surprisingly, we saw very few lights.

Flight attendants handed out warm, moist towels with which to freshen up. Excitedly we gathered together all our stuff so we'd be ready to deplane. We could barely contain our enthusiasm as we waited for the plane to land. We were on a trip that was a dream come true for both of us. Then, at virtually the same time, we said to each other, "We need to pray!" Both of us had suddenly felt the grip of fear and anxiety. We recognized that kind of fear, and we knew it was not of the Lord. Instantly, we turned to each other and grabbed one another's hands. Right then and there, seated near the back of the plane, we began to pray. We prayed that the Lord would chase away what seemed like a mountain of fear, as well as our doubt and lack of peace. We asked that He would help us put our trust in Him every step of the way and that He would send His holy angels to protect us. We prayed that He would shower us with His wisdom and knowledge, that we would have joy, and that we would know His peace that passes all our own understanding. Immediately, a great sense of relief came over us! This act of stopping what we were doing and praying didn't seem strange at all. Both of us had been doing this together for years. We knew God was the One who had allowed us to be on this trip, and we desperately needed His help.

Barbara and I had gone on previous mission trips to other countries, and these trips were always intense. We made these trips with people we knew well. Now we would be traveling with people we didn't know. Barbara had met Bob and Kathy only once before, at a Bible Conference. After meeting Barbara, Bob and Kathy felt led to invite her to travel with them and to speak at a number of places on this trip. In many ways, Barbara and I would be traveling with strangers in a strange land. We were walking by faith, not by sight! The words God had initially given me, when I prayerfully sought His counsel about going on this trip, kept resonating in my head: *Have I not commanded you? Be strong and courageous. Do not be terrified; do not be discouraged, for the LORD your God will be with you wherever you go.* (Joshua 1:9) This promise from God caused His peace to fill my heart. As our plane descended, I kept repeating these words in my mind: *Don't be afraid. I am with you wherever you go. You are not alone.* I knew that God was putting this trip together like a puzzle, one piece at a time! With my mind's eye, I had imagined it would look one way. But I also knew that, as so often happens with God, the final picture might end up looking far different. Then, with a hard thump, and a jolt, our plane landed.

Hastily, Barbara and I made our way off the plane and stood in a very long line to get our visas. We tried hard not to stare at the police with automatic weapons in hand as they scanned the sea of people with their trained eyes. Eventually we obtained our visas and made our way through customs. As men in uniforms rummaged through our carry-on bags, we prayed that nothing would be confiscated. We breathed a big sigh of relief and gave thanks to God when He got us through without anything being taken. Then we began the hours-long process of arranging safe transportation for us, our luggage, and the thirty large containers filled with the many donated items we had brought with us on this trip.

The next morning, Barbara and I lay almost motionless in a dingy motel room in Nairobi. I had slept very little during the night. The last thing I remember from the night before was trying not to choke as I pulled a dust-filled mosquito netting around Barbara. These nettings were meant to protect us from malaria-carrying mosquitos. Barbara had fallen asleep almost immediately. Waving the dust away, I struggled with my own netting and tried not to think about who had slept on the sheets before me or what else might be living in the sheets. As the noises of the night crept through the openings of the barred windows, I prayed until I fell into a restless sleep.

A few hours later, we were awakened by the loud sound of a horn blowing. It was 4:00 a.m. We learned later that this horn was blown every morning and at other times throughout the day, calling Muslims to prayer. I groggily pushed back the netting and headed off to a small room. This room had rough and uneven cement floors, with a hole in the ground. This hole was the toilet. I was determined not to bemoan the circumstances as I learned how to negotiate the process of squatting close to the ground and balancing just right, while at the same time struggling not to let my clothing, or the small roll of toilet paper I clutched in my hand, touch the wet and grimy areas around the hole. Trying hard not to breathe in all the smells wafting around the tiny room, I kept thinking, *It could be worse.* I knew I had to focus on the good things. Almost immediately, the thought popped into my mind, *Thank you, Lord, that this toilet room has a door with a latch on it!*

A gleam of sunlight was creeping through the window, so we could see dimly enough to get ourselves ready for the five-hour drive to our first destination in Kenya: Nyahururu. I prayed that the Lord would show me which skirt I should wear for the day. This would become a daily practice for me on the rest of the trip. I felt impressed by the Lord to wear a skirt that my sister, Jan, had sent with me. She had our itinerary. I knew that she, being a prayer warrior, would be interceding for us at that very hour. This was comforting to me, like an "armor of prayer" wrapped around me. How good the Lord was to lead me to wear her skirt that day! After we were dressed, Barbara and I continued our practice of reading the Bible and praying aloud together. We asked the Lord for His guidance and safety. We also prayed that He would help us to be ready and willing to respond to His Spirit's leading.

We found Sammy waiting for us outside the hotel, smiling from ear to ear. Sammy was the nineteen-year-old son of a pastor named Weston, and his wife, Violet. Pastor Weston and Violet ran a large orphanage in Nyahururu. We would be staying in their home during our time there. I liked Sammy immediately when he met us at the airport the night before and welcomed us to Kenya. That morning he had secured a small bus large enough to accommodate us, our luggage, and our thirty large containers. Even though we had to ride in a rickety old bus, I thanked the Lord we had a higher vantage point from which we could see everything in this land that I had dreamed of so long ago.

The roughly paved roads were narrow and full of potholes. I was surprised to see so many brilliantly colored flowers, like magenta bougainvillea, growing wild along the countryside. Scampering monkeys, baboons, and other African wildlife roamed freely across the roads, often causing traffic delays. We had to stop at many checkpoints, necessitating us keeping our passports, visas, and identification cards handy as weapon-carrying soldiers came aboard to carry out inspections. At one checkpoint, we were escorted off the bus and waited as they went through our containers and luggage. Silently we prayed that they would not seize any of our things. Gradually I began to calm down and take a few deep breaths, remembering God's promise to take care of me wherever I went.

We finally arrived in Nyahururu, a town with a population of 35,000. As we drove through the town, I noticed scores of people were walking barefooted along the road, carrying very large containers on the top of their heads. These containers held food, their water for the day, or other necessary items. Many others were riding bicycles with items on their heads as well. Our bus turned off the semi-paved road onto a red-colored, deeply rutted dirt road. We held onto to the seats in front of us as we bounced along, the driver dodging deep ridges and holes in the road. A few minutes later, we pulled up in front of the home of Pastor Westin and Violet.

Pastor Westin and Violet's house was a safe-haven home leased by people in the United States for them and their family to live in. It also housed many visitors like us who would come from all over the world. That very weekend, we were among dozens of Americans who were staying there. There was a large Bible-teaching conference taking place in Nyahururu. At the culmination of the conference, there would be a graduation of African nationals who had taken classes for two years to become pastors or Bible teachers. Hundreds of Africans from the community were also attending the conference, hungry to be taught Biblical truths.

Sitting in the bus, I could see a high cement wall that surrounded Westin and Violet's two-story home. The top of this wall was laden with shards of sharp broken glass. A heavy metal gate, secured with numerous locks, guarded the entrance into a small courtyard inside the walls. We disembarked from the bus in front of the gate. Stepping into the red, gooey, claylike mud, we gingerly carried our bags into the courtyard. Upon entering the door of the house, we removed our mud-caked shoes. We were told that some of the orphans who had been rescued by Pastor Weston and Violet, and who served as house-maids, would clean our shoes and bring them to us.

After shedding our shoes and coats, we walked slowly down a cold and dark cement hallway, allowing our eyes to adjust to the dim light. Even though the house was wired for electricity, they had no control over when the electricity would be on and when it would be off. Now it was off. At the end of the hall, straight ahead of us, I could make out a tiny room. The size of a very small walk-in closet, it was called a "kitchen." In this room was a woman, squatted on the cement floor, cooking over a large metal tray that held burning coals. Her name was Sheba, a widow with children, whose husband had died of AIDS. She was the cook, taken in by Violet and Pastor Weston, and was given room and board for herself and her children.

And then we met Violet. She welcomed us graciously and asked one of the orphan girls, Jane, to prepare a cup of chai, or tea, for us. We found a place to sit in a large meeting room to the right of the kitchen. Mix-matched sofas and chairs ran all around the walls of the entire room. Obviously it was meant to be a gathering place for a lot of people. We finished our chai, and Jane took us up some cement steps to our room on the second story. It was almost like a dorm room, filled with many twin-sized beds. After looking over the room, Barbara and I took time to get settled and also spent time reading our Bibles and praying together. We knew the next few days would be very intense with a jam-packed schedule.

The rest of the evening was a blur of activity. Groups of people came and went, all getting ready for the next day's conference and graduation. I tried hard to remember names and faces. Finally, around midnight, we slipped under our sheets, knowing the sound of the horn would wake us at the 4:00 a.m. hour. As I prayed quietly under the bedsheets, I suddenly thought, *Oh, no, I didn't give a skirt away!* Almost immediately I sensed the Lord saying to me, *I will tell you what to do and when to do it.*

With roosters crowing and cows mooing Barbara and I woke, right as the prayer horn was blowing. Through the open-barred windows, I could smell the smoke of a wood fire already burning. Other guests in the house were still sleeping as I quietly headed downstairs to the "kitchen" looking for coffee. I stuck my head in and saw Sheba frying tortilla-like pieces of bread in a sea of oil and Violet cutting up some papaya. I didn't recognize Violet at first—she was not wearing her wig from the day before—but I recognized her sweet, gentle voice. I took advantage of the opportunity to talk with her and to learn more about her, as well as to help set up the food for breakfast.

As I spent this time with Violet, I was touched by how she oversaw all of the activities of the house. She treated the orphaned boys and girls who worked there with heartfelt love and respect, working alongside of them and not demanding to be waited upon. I admired her kind nature as well as her ability to stay calm with so many things going on in her very busy household. She clearly had the peace of Jesus ruling in her heart! This was all the more significant to me when I learned what Violet had gone through as a pastor's wife, a mother, a teacher, and a servant of the Lord. She was surrounded by danger every day. She had faced some extraordinarily difficult and fear-provoking circumstances in her life. Just the year before, her ten-year-old son had been senselessly murdered while he was playing right outside the walls of their home.

Violet faced fear every day—fear of bodily danger, life-threatening illnesses, robbery and vandalism. Yet, in the face of these fears, she remained a woman of prayer who faithfully and diligently called upon the Lord. Drawing strength from Jesus, she courageously acted upon the promises of His Word, not the fears of her heart. I instinctively knew that Violet and I had a connection. We both were teachers. We both had lost sons. We both were women of prayer. We both were looking to Jesus to deal with our fears. But I sensed that there was another connection that the Lord had in mind. I didn't know what it was, but I knew that the Lord was guiding me a step at a time. And, over the next few days, He would reveal to me exactly what that connection was.

I hurried back upstairs, praying that God would impress me with the skirt I should wear for the day. With haste and anticipation, I quickly threw myself together and hurried back downstairs. The bus was waiting to take a group of us to the Bible conference and graduation ceremony.

When we arrived for the Bible conference, hundreds of Kenyans were already gathered in a large warehouse that had been rented for the weekend's events. We observed them singing and worshipping the Lord with a great freedom and enthusiasm like we'd never seen before. This certainly was a tiny foretaste of what Heaven might be like! At the end of the day's conference, Barbara and I—along with other guests and speakers—were asked to lay hands on, and pray over, each one of the graduates. It was a wonderful beginning to our weeks of ministry together in Africa.

The following day was a Sunday. Barbara and I were invited to spend time with Nancy and Esther, two widows who were serving together in an exciting ministry to women in Nyahururu. It turned out to be such a full and rewarding day, and it gave us the opportunity to minister in their church. We planned to have more time with Nancy and Esther in the days to come.

The next day, Monday, turned out to be one of those days I'll remember the rest of my life. Still exhausted from the events of the day before, I sat up in bed as the 4:00 a.m. horn sounded. Barbara was already dressed in her *"clowning" attire,* as she would be ministering to hundreds of children and teachers in Pastor Westin and Violet's orphanage. I propped up my little flashlight so that I could read my Bible, write down what had happened the previous day, and pray. Barbara and I went over what she'd be doing that day and how I could assist her. For years we'd worked together well; we were anticipating, with much joy, the blessing of sharing with children at the orphanage. We sang worship songs and excitedly prayed, and then Barbara headed out the door. I quickly washed up with bottled water, a bar of soap, and a washcloth I'd brought from home. Having already prayed, I knew immediately which skirt I should wear. It was a skirt belonging to Connie, a "behind the scenes" praying kind of gal. Even though it was way too big for me, I didn't question why I should wear it; I just put it on.

All at once I heard the most horrific scream. I ran downstairs and out into the courtyard, where Barbara was wailing and saying, *"No, no, no!"* She was walking in circles in the soggy red mud. Through her sobs I learned she had just received news that her mother had suddenly died the day before. She would need to go back to California right away for the funeral. Barbara stopped circling, put her hands on my shoulders, and looked straight into my eyes. She asked, *"Are you going back with me or are you going to stay here?"*

I looked at her and said, *"I really need to go and pray about this."*

I hurried back up to our room; wrestling with fear and sadness, I cried out to the Lord. *What should I do? I need your help. Lord, I need to know—NOW!* My prayer was an urgent call, like dialing up 9-1-1. I was desperately asking for a word from the Lord so I would know what to do. I began to be overwhelmed with a feeling of His presence. And then, boom! Just like that, Joshua 1:9 once again popped into my mind, *Have I not commanded you? Be strong and courageous. Do not be terrified; do not be discouraged, for the LORD your God will be with you wherever you go.* Words kept bubbling up in my heart: *Do not be afraid! Did I not say to you that I am able? Didn't I say that you would have ALL that you need when you need it, and that I'd be with you always? That very morning God had prepared me for this moment as I had* read Deuteronomy 28:1–14 in my Bible. This passage was about the blessings of obeying God and following His commands, and held this promise from God: *"The LORD will make you the head, not the tail. If you pay attention to the commands of the LORD your God that I give you this day and carefully follow them, you will always be at the top, never at the bottom."* (Deuteronomy 28:13) Now I seemed to hear God say these words in my heart: *Stay put! You are to be the head and not the tail!* Amazingly, I had an indescribable sense of peace. I knew that the entirety of my life had been a preparation for this moment. I was to stay in Africa and take up Barbara's role.

As I left my room and walked back to the courtyard to tell Barbara, my heart was flooded with mixed feelings and emotions. I felt a great sadness and heartache for Barbara's loss of her mother. I felt the shock of fear and concern over the uncertainty of what was ahead. I would have several more weeks in Africa, traveling in four different countries with people I barely knew; nevertheless, I had the strong assurance of what God was saying to me in His Word. I wouldn't have my longtime friend Barbara with me, but I would have my best Friend, Jesus, with me.

Barbara had just a few hours before she needed to leave for the airport. In spite of all that she was facing, she still wanted to go to the orphanage to minister to the children who were there. Esther arrived to drive Barbara and me to the orphanage. I climbed into the backseat, followed by Barbara who was dressed in oversized clowning clothes and shoes, a big red nose, and humongous hot-pink glasses. We scrunched close together in Esther's tiny car for the bumpy ride to the orphanage. More than ever Barbara still desired to share with the children, in spite of her deep sadness over the sudden death of her mother. She had something in common with the children we would be seeing. They, too, were experiencing pain, loss, and separation from someone they deeply loved. We bounced up and down in silence as Esther drove us down the dirt roads. Just an hour earlier the Lord had led us to sing together a worship song praising the name of Jesus based on Psalm 18: *"The Lord is my rock, my fortress and my deliverer; my God is my rock, in whom I take refuge." (Psalm 18:2)* I took Barbara's hand and prayed that the Lord would enable her to laugh and have fun with the kids, that He would help her do exactly what He wanted her to do, and that He would bless her with His presence and strength.

We could hear the children cheering and shouting as Esther turned into the gates of the orphanage. Suddenly a sea of little faces surrounded her car, as hundreds of children poured out of their huts and ran to greet us. They were cheering, *"Welcome! Welcome!" In the time that followed, it was beautiful to see* how God spoke through Barbara with her playful tricks and mime routines, giving her incredible strength. She brought the children much joy, love, and laughter. In the face of all that she was going through and all that was ahead of her, she prayerfully acted upon the promises of God's Word. He, in turn, blessed her with strength to do what she did and granted her the desires of her heart.

Barbara having fun with the kids at the orphanage.

As the bus rolled away carrying Barbara to Nairobi, I stood on the dusty red grounds of the orphanage and watched until it was out of sight. I felt numb, almost frozen with fear. Certainly this was not the plan I had. My friend was gone. I suddenly felt very alone. In my mind I thought, *Lord, what have I done? Did I hear you right? Did I do the right thing by staying here? Please help me! I can't possibly do this without Barbara.* Just like that, as I called out to God in prayer, I was once again overwhelmed with a sense of peace. Even though I did not fully understand everything that was to come, I was beginning a journey. And this journey was one that would fulfill the dream that had been birthed in my heart when I was a little girl back in Texas.

With tears still in my eyes, I turned around. Before I could say anything, many sweet orphans rushed up to me—giggling, hugging, grabbing my hands and pulling me to get in line with them for some lunch. I was given a bowl of food that resembled oatmeal; along with the children, I scooped it out of the bowl and ate it with my fingers. Gathering up my oversized skirt, I sat down on a narrow wooden bench and asked them to tell me their stories. All too soon, the sound of a clanging bell reverberated to get our attention. Immediately everyone stopped talking. Violet, in her role as director of the orphanage, stood up and summoned all the children and teachers to gather together inside a tent area.

To my surprise, Violet called me up to where she was standing and introduced me, telling the children that I was a teacher back in America. She asked me if I had a lesson to teach them. I thought to myself: *Really? No heads-up ahead of time? Can this be happening to me?* I stood there, fear again creeping up within me. It felt like this fear was trying to choke me. My mouth was dry. I surely must have had that *"deer in the headlights" look!* What could I possibly teach them? Thoughts tumbled around in my mind. All eyes were on me, waiting for me to speak. What should I say? Here it was—the moment I had been waiting for! Had not God said to me, *"You will have all that you need when you need it"?* In my mind and heart I prayed, *I do need you, Lord. Give me a word. Let me be your mouthpiece.* That's when a thought came to me. I could tell them about my childhood dream—a dream to come to Africa and teach!

I opened my mouth and started to speak with boldness. This boldness just rose up within me. I knew it was divine strength from God's Spirit Himself, enabling me to speak the words He wanted me to say. I told them that regardless of their circumstances or whatever had happened to them in their past, they could still have a dream. I was living proof that such God-given dreams could happen to people. I explained to them how Barbara, the funny clown lady, was supposed to have been the one teaching them, not me. But now she was gone. And, unexpectedly, I was teaching instead of her. Even though I was very sad for what had happened to my friend, God was bringing good out of it. He was allowing my dream to come true, the dream He had given me as a child to teach in Africa. After many years of waiting, here I was living out that dream!

A dream come true for Donna!

I could see the children listening attentively as the Lord led me to get very practical with them. Just for fun I told them to think about, or imagine, some dream—a thought or idea that, for now, might seem totally unattainable. To them, it might be an "impossible dream." Then I asked them to write their dream or idea in notebooks they had just been given. They could simply start by writing what they wanted to be when they grew up or places where they wanted to go beyond the gates of the orphanage. "Think big!" I said, "Have fun imagining." Words were just spilling out of me as I felt God giving me ideas of what to say to them. I shared with them how I prayed as a little girl about going to Africa. I assured them God had a plan and purpose for their lives, and that no matter what had happened to them in the past, it was no surprise to God. He was able to bring good out of everything in their lives! I told them that they were all precious and important to Him. I encouraged them to love God with all their hearts, to pray to Him, and to not give up hope. I reminded them that just as He was helping me to trust in Jesus, he would also help them. Then I led them in prayer.

When I finished I saw the children's eyes dance with excitement as their hands flew up. They were filled with delight and wanted to tell me what they had written down! I was thrilled to see how quickly so many of them had responded. Even though Violet dismissed them for "free time," many of them hung around to show me their notebooks. They asked me many questions about how I ended up being able to come to Africa. I could see that they were on the road to their own dreams! The Lord had given me a message they needed to hear. Looking back on it now, I know I experienced the moving of God's Spirit in and through me that day, and also the blessing and fulfillment of my own childhood dream. God is good!

That evening, after helping Sheba and Violet with dinner, I excused myself and went upstairs. I needed time alone to process what had happened that day. My emotions had been all over the map since the phone call Barbara had received about the death of her mother. Feeling a bit shaken I sat down on my bed, in what had previously been "our" room. But now I was all by myself. How could I possibly do this? Reality was settling in. A tidal wave of self-pity seemed to wash over me. I knew I needed to confess that right away. I also knew I absolutely needed quiet time—time to seek after the Lord's counsel in His Word and in prayer.

I recalled how immediately His words had come to me that morning, as I cried out to God, asking Him whether I should stay or go home with Barbara. My prayer had been a cry for help, and He had answered me quickly! *Stay put! You are to be the head and not the tail!* It wasn't an audible voice that I heard. Instead, in response to my prayer for help, God's Spirit brought back to my mind a verse from the Bible I had read earlier that morning.

In that very moment I was experiencing what King Solomon talked about when He prayed, *"May He not leave us or forsake us, that He may incline our hearts to Him, to walk in all His ways...."* (1 Kings 8:57–58 ESV) I knew that the Holy Spirit lives in the heart of every person who knows Jesus as their Savior, and that He wants to "incline" our inner being toward the things of God, leading us and guiding us. I had learned, and was still learning, how to follow these inclinations—which can come from from a Bible verse, a line in a hymn, a word of counsel from another Christian, or even an inner impression that just doesn't go way. Solomon wrote in Proverbs 3:5–6, *"Trust in the Lord with all your heart, and do not lean on your own understanding; in all your ways acknowledge Him, and He will make your paths straight."* God's Spirit had graciously been teaching me how to "acknowledge Him"—to read the Word, pray, listen, and wait for Him to guide me in what to do. Thankfully I had discovered that whenever God's Spirit inclined my heart to Him in this way, I would eventually experience a sense of peace and direction. I was holding on for dear life to His promise that this time would be no different!

Thinking about the fears that I had to face, I expressed my gratitude to God for the assurance of His love in Romans 5:5, which says: *"God has poured out His love into our hearts by the Holy Spirit, who He has given us."* I understood that this was a love that only God can give. With the help of His Holy Spirit, I decided to incline my heart to the truth of 1 John 4:18: *"There is no fear in love. But perfect love drives out fear."*

So I sat in my room, gradually coming to a greater awareness that even though I was feeling lonely, I was definitely NOT alone. I said in my heart, *Thank You, Lord, that I took time to read the Bible this morning, instead of just rushing downstairs. Keep me close to You. Keep speaking to me in Your Word. Help me to fix my eyes on You, to rely on You and Your perfect love, not on myself. Help me to hear from you, moment by moment. Incline my heart toward You.* At that moment I felt like Samuel must have felt when he said to the Lord, *"Speak, for your servant is listening."* (1 Samuel 3:10) I wanted to—no, I needed to—hear His voice in the hours, days, and weeks ahead.

After getting myself ready for bed, I lay down. The schedule inevitably had to change after Barbara left. I wished I could talk to my husband, but knew I couldn't. So I continued talking to the Lord about many, many things. As I listened quietly, God's Spirit began to put thoughts in my mind. I started to think about the next day. I wasn't sure which skirt to wear, but I had a sense that the Lord would let me know. Before long, I had fallen asleep.

Very early the next morning, even before the blowing of the horn, Violet knocked on my door, telling me that a bus from the orphanage would soon be arriving to pick us up for a special trip. This day was to be a day of fun—an adventure! Violet, Sammy, Kathy, Bob and I, along with the eighth grade class from Violet's orphanage, were making a five-hour journey to the Ol Pejeta Conservancy. This would be a once-in-a-lifetime experience for them, and for us, giving all of us an opportunity to observe many of the animals of Kenya in their protected habitat. This conservancy, located between Mt. Kenya and the Aberdare Mountain Range, consisted of 90,000 acres of savanna rangeland, groves of acacia trees, brush, and vegetation growing along rivers. It was also home to what is called "Africa's Big Five"—buffalos, elephants, leopards, lions, and rhinoceroses. In addition to that, the conservancy was also home to thousands of other wild mammals and over 570 recorded species of birds.

Because the early morning air was quite chilly, I knew immediately which skirt to wear, with my warm knit pants underneath it. I put on every layer of clothing I possibly could. Sheba handed me a hot cup of chai and a biscuit as I boarded the bus. The tea slowly began to warm me up. It wasn't long before we arrived at the gates of the orphanage. In the still of the cool morning air, we could hear the laughter and voices of the children. Very few of them had ever been away from the orphanage, and they were all keyed up with excitement and anticipation. They joyfully crowded on the bus, and soon we were headed off to the conservancy.

It was very dark and still early; after several rounds of robust singing and quiet chitchat, the kids' voices slowly became muffled. Most of them fell asleep. Having been told we'd have a greater chance to see more animals at the watering holes in the cool of the morning, rather than in the heat of the day, we'd decided to leave long before sunrise. It proved to be a great decision. On the way we were blessed with seeing a spectacular sunrise of oranges, reds, pinks and yellows, with Mt. Kilimanjaro off in the distant clouds. These were awe-inspiring views to take in, and I spent much of the trip giving thanks to God for the beauty of His creation.

Upon our arrival at the conservancy, we got our tickets. Violet, Sammy, the teachers and the children had free tickets because they were nationals. It cost the rest of us a relatively small fee of only $30.00 for the entire day. It was money well spent! We were all able to be together on the same bus and had the most enthusiastic, story-telling guide of all time! Appropriately, his name was Solomon. He was passionate, as well as knowledgeable, about all the animals and also about preserving them from extinction and poaching in this safe environment. We were dumbfounded at the sheer numbers and varieties of mammals and birds. We snapped pictures of giraffes and zebras as they seemingly stopped "on cue" right in front of our bus for a photo op. I was glad that we were in a bus with glass windows, as the giraffes could have easily stuck their heads right inside the bus. There were herds and herds of elephants, hyenas, cattle, buffalo, antelope, leaping gazelles, and rhinos. Not only that, there were many smaller animals, including foxes, warthogs, dogs, otters, monkeys, squirrels and hares. Birds of every size and kind, too many to count, lingered around the watering holes. I thought one watering hole was pink, but it only appeared that way because literally thousands of pink flamingoes surrounded the water. It was so moving to see the look on the students' faces as they gazed in amazement at all the animals—especially as they watched eagles soar majestically into the sky. All of us were excited when we finally spotted some mother lions and their cubs while they were napping in the brush. What a thrill! These eighth graders were literally seeing the animals of their country for the very first time.

Every so often we would get off the bus for a walking adventure. During one of these times, I had an opportunity to speak with

Solomon. It turned out that he was a Christian who was married and had a young child at home. As we talked, Solomon leaned his weapon against a tree and pulled out from his pocket a picture of his family. He told me how blessed he was to have such a good job and how he enjoyed telling people about all the animals God had made. He wanted to provide for his family and work hard for them so they would be proud of him. Upon our return to the front entrance of the conservancy, Solomon paid us many compliments on the behavior of the children. He was amazed at how they displayed very good manners and were respectful to him, listening attentively as he talked. I would definitely concur with that! After a late afternoon lunch of jam-on-a-biscuit and some water, we were on the road again for our trip back to Nyahururu.

I was able to sit next to Violet all the way home. I mentioned Solomon's comments and told her how proud she should be of her kids. Having hours to talk, I asked her about her life, whereupon she told me stories of her growing up years, her adventurous past and how she and Pastor Westin met. She wanted to know of my past, my family and life in America. As we shared back and forth, I knew the Lord was deepening our relationship. Our conversation turned from little facts and stories about ourselves to deeper things. We talked for a long time about our fears, our family concerns, support-ing and encouraging our pastor-husbands, loneliness, finding friends, finances, dealing with grief over the loss of a child, the oneness of our faith, and the importance of taking time for prayer and Bible study. I was struck by how much we had in common as women. We lived on different continents, in different cultures, with different skin colors, yet we had the same feelings, fears, and challenges. Even more impor-tantly, we shared a mutual bond—Jesus! We both agreed that it was God's amazing love in Christ that brought us together through the power of His Spirit. We laughed, cried, and talked all the way back to Nyahururu.

Later that evening, after cleaning up from dinner, Violet and I sat for a very long time around the cooking pot Sheba brought in from the kitchen to keep us warm. The room was dark and chilly, with the sound of the wind whistling through a broken window. As we huddled together near the steaming pot, we talked about the day's trip to the conservancy, all the animals we'd seen, and the immense joy it had given the kids. What a whirlwind of a day! Then we moved on to Barbara's departure and shared with each other how deeply it affected us and the children at the orphanage. We sat quietly for a while, thinking in silence.

Because the fire had gone out from the cooking pot, we wrapped some blankets around us. Violet and I leaned in toward each other and shared more stories about being a wife, a mother, and a teacher. It was evident that God had bought us together for a very special moment in time, and we would cherish it forever. The warmth of the coals had long since cooled off when I pulled out a bag containing the oversized skirt I'd worn that day. I told Violet how the Lord had impressed it in my mind and in my heart to give her the skirt. God had used her to allow me to teach the children at the orphanage, and in turn this skirt was to be a "thank you" blessing for her. I showed Violet the label that was pinned inside with the name of the woman who had given the skirt. She was also a teacher. I asked Violet to remember her whenever she wore the skirt. I encouraged her to recall the way God had used her to bless me, thereby making my childhood dream come true. Now I wanted to bless her with the gift of this skirt. That day we had connected, and the skirt would be a reminder of our friendship, as well as how God has a way of bringing good out of every event in our lives. His perfect love would always conquer our fears. We were both moved to tears. After praying together, we hugged each other and said good night. The next morning when I went into the kitchen, Violet was wearing the skirt. It fit her perfectly!

If you want to pray, listen, and respond to God…
In the face of fear, call upon God right away and be willing to
act upon His Word, not your fears.

Violet is on the left, wearing Donna's skirt; Sheba is on the right, wearing Barbara's skirt.

CHAPTER TWO - REFLECTION PAGES

"Call upon God right away and be willing to act upon His Word, not your fears."

PRAY AND LISTEN TO GOD AS YOU READ THESE WORDS FROM THE BIBLE

2 Timothy 1:7
For God did not give us a spirit of timidity, but a spirit of power, of love and of self-discipline.

2 Corinthians 12:9a
But he said to me, "My grace is sufficient for you, for my power is made perfect in weakness."

Philippians 4:6-7
Do not be anxious about anything, but in everything, by prayer and petition, with thanksgiving, present your requests to God. And the peace of God, which transcends all understanding, will guard your hearts and minds in Christ Jesus.

Psalm 34:4
I sought the LORD, and he answered me; he delivered me from all my fears.

Psalm 41:10
So do not fear, for I am your God. I will strengthen you and help you; I will uphold you with my righteous right hand.

Ephesians 6:16–17
In addition to all this, take up the shield of faith, with which you can extinguish all the flaming arrows of the evil one. Take the helmet of salvation and the sword of the Spirit, which is the word of God.

Hebrews 11:6
And without faith it is impossible to please God, because anyone who comes to him must believe that he exists and that he rewards those who earnestly seek him.

QUESTIONS FOR REFLECTION AND DISCUSSION

1. What almost sabotaged Donna's dream of teaching in Africa, and what was her immediate response to Barbara's news?

2. Describe a time when you felt worried, upset, or afraid. How did you deal with it?

3. What are your greatest fears today?

4. Read the story of Elijah and his fears in 1 Kings 19:1–19 in your Bible. What can you learn from these verses about how to react in the face of your fears?

5. Why do you think prayer makes such a difference in dealing with fear?

6. What role does faith play in acting upon God's Word, not your fears? Does such faith seem risky to you?

7. What was something that inspired and encouraged you in this first skirt story, and what will you be praying for as a result of it?

PRAYER OF RESPONSE

Dear Jesus, I acknowledge You as my Prince of Peace and the One who is the Way, the Truth, and the Life. Thank You that You promise to give me eyes to see Your truth and ears to hear Your voice. When I am doubting, afraid or worried, please help me to stop what I am doing and turn to You in prayer right away. Move me to seek after You, to wait and really listen. Show me what You want me to do and grant me grace to let go of my own ideas of dealing with my fears. Fill me with faith to act upon Your Word, instead of acting on the basis of my anxiety. I name my fears to You right now and give them to You...... I praise You for Your perfect love that drives out all fear. By the power of Your Holy Spirit, I take up the shield of faith, I put on the helmet of salvation, and I wield the sword of Your Word, confident that You will help me grow in a new life of praying, listening, and responding to God. In Your life-giving, peace-giving name I pray. Amen!

SKIRT STORY NUMBER TWO— CATHERINE

If you want to pray, listen, and respond to God...
When God asks you to do something you wouldn't ordinarily do,
obey Him even when it doesn't make sense to you.

After Barbara's departure on Monday, the original plans we had for the remaining days of our first week in Africa changed significantly. As so often happens, we had one plan but God had another. Following our return from the animal conservancy, Bob, Kathy, and I revamped our schedule. We spent the next few days visiting hospitals, prisons, and several small orphanages in and around Nyahururu.

On Thursday evening, knowing we'd see Violet again on our way back from Uganda, we said our quick goodbyes and left for the bus station. Sammy got us there just in time to catch the bus to Mombasa, Kenya, over 400 miles southeast of Nyahururu.

Most of the fifteen-hour bus ride to Mombasa was made in the darkness of night. I didn't know how anyone could sleep because of the unrelenting jolts from the driver dodging potholes in the road, frequent stops for inspections, and occasional delays when we came to large tree branches that had been laid across the roadway by drivers to signal a broken down vehicle or some other problem. On top of all of that, the driver continually played music videos with the volume turned all the way up. *Help me, Lord,* I prayed.

As the night wore on and my eyes grew accustomed to the darkness, I looked out the window and saw a number of wild animals walking near the roadway, including several large lions. I was taken aback as I realized that many Africans were also walking for miles along this very same road, in the ink-black darkness of the night. They continually faced the daily fears and ongoing danger of these wild animals. A chill ran right down my spine. Prior to being on this trip, I had not given much thought to all the struggles and dangerous conditions so many people on this continent had to deal with each day just to survive. In my heart I prayed, *Lord, keep me mindful of these things and show me Your purposes in and through them all. Give me a teachable heart to learn the lessons You want to reveal to me each and every day. Help me never to take my safety for granted, and make me aware of people who don't have Your peace.* In the days to come, God would answer this prayer in ways I could not have imagined at the time. The lessons that lay ahead for me would change my life forever.

We arrived in Mombasa late Friday morning, fatigued and exhausted from our journey. Mombasa is the second largest city in Kenya, made up of a predominately Muslim population exceeding one million people. Located right on the coast of the Indian Ocean, it is Kenya's only large seaport. As we drove through the city, we prayed, *"Lord, lead us where to stay."* And He did! We drove past several beautiful, expensive-looking, luxury hotels and then saw an older, less expensive-looking, run-down hotel, right on the white sandy beaches of the ocean. We stopped at this hotel and negotiated a good price for a stay of three nights and four days. One of the workers at the hotel took us to a two-story building, complete with a thatched roof, surrounded by coconut palms, exotic tropical plants, and blooming purple jacaranda trees. We were given the upstairs quarters of this building, which had two bedrooms. Best of all, these quarters had a small bathroom complete with an inside toilet. There was also a large balcony outfitted with an outdoor barbecue, cookware and utensils, so we could do our own cooking. And we had a beautiful ocean front view, courtesy of the Lord!

The next day was Saturday. Rather than being tourists, we took a good part of the day in Bible study and prayer. We needed to rearrange our itinerary and redo our budget for our remaining time in Africa. Barbara had been a large supporter for our trip, but her unexpected departure changed our financial situation significantly. When we arrived in Africa, each of us had exchanged a major portion of our funds into Kenyan paper money called shillings. We needed to budget wisely to make sure these funds would last for the remainder of our trip.

That evening, Violet's husband, Pastor Weston, came over for a visit. He had arrived earlier that week from Nyahururu to direct a conference for Christian leaders being held nearby. Pastor Weston asked us to go to one of the larger churches in the city of Mombasa, made up of some of the working professionals and leaders in the community. We were to participate in their Sunday morning worship service as part of this conference. A friend of Pastor Weston named Angelo pastored this church. Bob and Kathy had been invited to speak there, and this was an unexpected open door for them. Together we thanked the Lord for such an opportunity!

Early Sunday morning, I sat on my bed and looked beyond the balcony of my room at the beautiful blue waters of the Indian Ocean. I felt a warm and gentle breeze blowing through the screens of the room. In the distance I could see fishermen, already coming in with their catch for the day. Tourists were beginning to lay down colorful towels, reserving a spot on the gorgeous beach. Families were splashing and playing while searching for seashells in the incredibly bathtub-warm water of the ocean. Because it was Sunday morning, there were more locals than usual on the beach. Some were bringing out camels for rides. Others were setting out wares of brightly colored clothing, paintings, jewelry, carved wooden figurines, and all sorts of touristy items. Still others were cooking up tasty spicy foods. I was drinking it all in with my eyes, when a couple of monkeys jumped down from the branch of a tree that was protruding through the old wooden bamboo decking of the balcony. They were scampering around and chasing one another. I thought about how amazingly bold they had become over the past few days of our stay. I'm sure my feeding them bits of food contributed to their ease in peeking through the screens of my door and tilting their heads at me, as if to say, *Where's the food, lady?*

I was thankful we had taken time the day before for much-needed rest, planning and prayer. The Lord surely had brought us to this quiet, yet beautiful place. I longed to join the many tourists I saw relaxing on the shores of the Indian Ocean, but I was immediately brought back to my Bible study and prayer time. Routinely now, I had been getting up at 4:00 a.m. to spend time in God's Word and prayer. Although I wasn't exactly sure what events lay ahead for the day, I knew I couldn't possibly go it alone without God's guidance. There had already been many times on this trip when I had asked the Lord for such guidance, praying, *What you say, Lord, I will do.*

Because Pastor Angelo's church was way across town, Pastor Weston had arranged transportation to take us there; it would be arriving soon. I quickly ate a breakfast bar I'd brought from America, took my vitamins and malaria pill, and drank from my bottled water. Now I had to hurry and get dressed. The previous evening, Kathy and I had chosen a number of skirts to put in a bag for Pastor Angelo's wife. As I was getting ready, I prayed once again, *"Lord, show me what skirt I should wear."* I had no idea which African woman I would be giving my skirt to that day, but I was trusting God to show me. I fingered through the stack of skirts in my suitcase. I was strangely drawn to a multicolored purple skirt and vest outfit. It was beautiful, with gold and silver threads woven throughout the gauze fabric. I read the small note pinned inside. A woman named Ann had given the skirt. She was a prayer warrior with a generous and giving heart. Confident I had heard from God, I put on the outfit. Being that it was way too big and too long for me, I folded over the waistband and safety-pinned the skirt on both sides. I was glad the vest and my black shirt covered up the lumps and bumps where it was pinned.

Earlier that morning, I had carefully counted out a small number of paper Kenyan schillings to put into the offering at the church. I tucked the schillings safely inside the pocket of my skirt. Then I put all the rest of my money—along with special valuables, my passport and my ID's—in a belt that I wrapped around my skirt and under my shirt. It was necessary to keep all our money and identification papers on our person at all times. Into my other pocket I put a tiny bottle of hand sanitizer and a small roll of toilet paper. I wanted to be prepared for everything.

Just as I was locking my suitcase, Kathy knocked on my door. She came in and handed me a large, floppy, purple hat to wear. Even though I didn't want to, I put it on anyway. I didn't know it at the time, but God would later use that purple hat for a special purpose. Right then, our car arrived. We slid two plastic containers—filled with things to give away—out our door and down the stairs, lifting them into the trunk. Grateful that we didn't have to arrange for transportation ourselves, we squeezed into the car and headed off to Pastor Angelo's church.

While we were on our way, Kathy received a call from Pastor Weston on her cell phone. He asked that I would also speak in church that morning. Panic immediately grabbed me right in my stomach. I thought to myself, *What? Me? Oh, my!* As quickly as one would snap her fingers, I lost all of my excitement and enthusiasm. Isn't that how it so often happens? My human nature was responding first. I was gripped with fear. I had already heard several of the American speakers deliver some awesome teachings at the Bible conference; a number of these speakers would be present at the church service. I suddenly felt very small and inadequate. My throat went dry and my body went limp; the "menopausal revenge sweat" began to slowly creep over me, from head to toe.

Sitting there in our cramped car, I silently thought: *Yikes, Lord! Why didn't you let me know this ahead of time, like when I was up at 4:00 a.m. this morning? I could have had time to prepare!* I certainly knew I needed to pray if I was ever going to do this. In my mind I said, *Lord, help me to calm down and focus.* I had memorized Philippians

4:6 many years ago. It came to mind right at that moment: *Do not be anxious about anything, but in everything, by prayer and petition, with thanksgiving, present your requests to God.* Bumping along the rugged roads of Mombasa, I stopped complaining and started praying. As I prayed, Joshua 1:9 slipped into my mind. *Have I not commanded you, be strong and courageous. Do not be terrified. Do not be discouraged. For the Lord your God will be with you wherever you go.* This message from Joshua was turning out to be my anchor verse in Africa. I was grateful God had planted it in my heart so many weeks before!

Without even moving my lips I prayed, *Lord, with your help, I will be strong. I will not be afraid. Show me what you want me to do.* The fear slowly began to lift as I focused on Him instead of my fears. Ahhhh … I could breathe again! I knew I needed to stay positive and set my mind on God's Word; I needed to remember how He had helped me and blessed me with His guidance in the past. So I began to thank Him for being faithful to me, for giving me messages when I had no time to plan, and for opening yet another door for me to speak, even though it had come unexpectedly. I was starting to understand what He meant in the word He'd given me from Deuteronomy 28:13, *"The LORD will make you the head, not the tail."* As I was thanking Him, a thought came into my mind: *I could share the same message that I gave earlier in the week at Esther and Nancy's church outside of Nyahururu. No one in Mombasa has heard it yet!* Taking a deep breath, I let out a huge sigh of relief. Now I knew what I would do. Or so I thought.

When we arrived, I climbed out of the car and headed off to a little shed behind the church called a "choo" in the Swahili language. In America, this kind of building would be called an outhouse. The big difference, however, was that in this shed there was nothing to sit on, only a hole in the ground. With toilet paper in one hand and yards of fabric from my long skirt in the other, I accomplished the maneuver. "Never again," I vowed, "will I ever complain when I have to wait in line to go to a restroom back home!"

While I was in the shed, I continued praying and gathering my thoughts. Then, right before I opened the door to step out, the Lord impressed me with these words: *Someone's coming to pray with you.* I got excited, picturing a nice, friendly, English-speaking African woman coming up to me and asking, "Can I pray with you?" However, when I stepped out of the shed, all I saw was a young boy whom I guessed to be about ten years old. He looked at me. I looked at him. And, just like that, I knew. It was as if God said, *It's him. He's the one you are to pray with.* So I walked right on over to him, stuck out my hand, and said, "Hi! I'm Miss Donna. What's your name?"

"James," he answered.

"James," I replied, "God sent you to pray with me. Would you pray with me?" James stood there staring at me in my purple hat, looking like he was in shock. He didn't say a word. I stared back at him, and said, "What the Lord tells me to do, I want to do!"

Then the Holy Spirit put it in my mind that James and I were to walk around the church building seven times, praying as we went. Back home, we called this kind of thing "prayer walking." Other times we would call it a "Joshua" march, referencing back to the Old Testament when God told the people of Israel to march around Jericho seven times. I had done this many times with people I knew well. But here I was, about to do it with someone I didn't know, at a church I had never been to before, in a land ten thousand miles from home.

We didn't have very long before the service was to begin. So I said to James, "I believe God wants us to pray out loud together as we walk around this church. And God wants us to go around this church not once, but seven times!" I grabbed him by the hand and off we went. I'm still amazed that he didn't take off running to get away from me—this funny-looking white woman wearing a huge long skirt and a floppy purple hat! But James stayed with me the entire time.

As the two of us began walking, I prayed that the Lord would give me the words He wanted me to say. Some of the things I prayed during those seven rounds of marching were: *"You are our Creator, our God. You are the Son of God. You are our Lord. You help us when we call out to You. You are our Guide. You listen to us. You rescue us. You are our King. You are our Deliverer. You are our Healer.   You give us hope. You are our Rock. You are our Refuge and Strength. You are able. You are the Bread of Life. You are Manna from heaven. You are our Provider. You are faithful. You are a very present help in trouble. You are merciful. You are our Comforter. You arose from the dead. You defeated our enemy. You are our Protector. You break apart strongholds. You open hearts. You are the Lamb of God. You are our Shepherd. You are our Redeemer. You are our Savior. You are our Peace. You are with us always. You work faith in our hearts. You are Beautiful. You are the Light of the World. You help us to worship You. You help us to give You honor and praise. You are our Teacher. You help us to learn. You help us to follow You. Hallelujah! Praise You, Father. Praise You, Jesus. Praise You, Spirit. Praise God from whom all blessings flow. Praise Him all creatures here below. Praise Him above you heavenly host. Praise Father, Son and Holy Ghost!"*

Simply put, I just spoke out words—attributes of God, truths from the Bible, and bits and pieces of spiritual songs and hymns. As God put them in my mind, I spoke them out. I prayed for things that came into my thoughts, things that I knew from the Bible were the will of God. While I don't remember singing, I might have, because I had done it in the past as I prayer-walked. I had discovered that the more you do it, the easier it gets—whether it's marching around the island in your kitchen at home or around a church in Africa. There is a Spirit-given freedom and abandonment that comes with confessing God's truth and God's will with your mouth. *"May the words of my mouth and the meditation of my heart be pleasing in your sight, O LORD, my Rock and my Redeemer."* (Psalm 19:14)

The locals continued arriving for church while James and I marched around the building praying. I can't even imagine what they were thinking as they watched us going around and around and around their church building. Not only was it a hot and sunny day, it was also a very humid day on the coast of the tropical Indian Ocean. I began to feel sweat beading up on my forehead and dripping down my spine under all my layers of clothing.

In spite of my discomfort, James and I kept going, circling the church seven times. I knew we had done exactly what the Lord had wanted us to do. Stopping near the entrance of the door to the church, I once again looked James right in his eyes and said, "James, I don't know all that was about, but I know the Lord sent you to walk and pray with me. Thank you!" I put my hand on his head and said, "May the Lord bless you always and give you His peace!" As James walked away, in my mind I asked the Lord, *Why in the world did You have me do that?* Before the morning was over, I would have my answer.

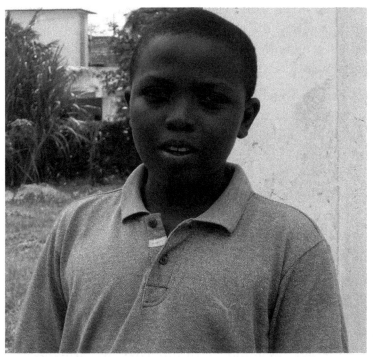

A picture of James taken before we walked and prayed seven times around the church.

Standing near the door of the church, I began to hear what had become more and more familiar to me—loud and vibrant African praise music. It was coming from inside, the rhythmic beat of the band's music summoning everyone to gather for worship. When I stepped through the door, I spotted Kathy. Taking me by my hand, she pulled me through the crowd and introduced me to Catherine, Pastor Angelo's wife. I liked her immediately. Catherine motioned for me to sit in a chair right next to her in the front row and whispered that she would be my interpreter. I felt comfortable knowing the Lord was bringing everything together, and I sensed His peace.

Pastor Angelo stepped onto the platform and welcomed everyone. When the band resumed playing, the people were out of their seats and onto their feet, worshipping God. The church was alive with motion. The enthusiasm of these African believers for singing and worshipping God was infectious. It was just plain impossible to stand still. I could see the joy on their faces and hear it in their loud singing. Recognizing a few of the choruses from our time in Nyahururu, I was able to sing along with them in their beautiful Swahili language. For me, it was one of the coolest things ever!

After Pastor Angelo shared some prayers, Bible readings, and a short message, it was time for the offering. I pulled out of my pocket the paper shillings I had set aside for this moment and waited for the basket to come. As I sat there, a voice inside me seemed to say, *Put in ALL your shillings.* That was nearly all the money I had for our trip, so I thought, Well, this surely isn't God's voice. He knows I don't have that kind of money to give away. *Certainly, God wouldn't want me to be stranded here with no money at all. Surely, He wouldn't ask me to give it all away!* But then the voice came again. *Put it ALL in.* When the basket arrived on my lap, I had a decision to make. So I did what any intelligent person with limited funds in a foreign country would do. I only put in the basket what I had earlier planned to give, and passed it on. No one was even the wiser about the jostling that had just taken place in my mind. But I immediately started feeling guilty about my decision.

When the offering was over, Pastor Angelo stepped up to the platform and introduced Kathy and Bob. I fought to listen to them as they gave their teaching. I was feeling sick at my stomach, uneasy and ill-equipped. I was struggling, no longer feeling at peace. Fear was gripping me.

After Kathy and Bob had finished their teaching, Catherine stepped up to the microphone and introduced me. My heart was pounding as I thought, *Surely, everyone must be seeing my nervousness!* With my Bible in one hand and lifting my bulky purple skirt with the other, I somehow made it up the steps. Unkempt and sweating from having circled the church seven times, I was still wearing that purple hat. My long and by now stringy-looking hair hung out from under the hat. As a woman who is usually put-together for church, I must have looked pretty pitiful. I began to tell them a little about myself and how I came to be in their country. However, it was as if my words were falling onto deaf ears. Catherine, my interpreter, looked over at me, patiently waiting for me to share my next thought. But I couldn't speak. There was complete silence. No words were coming to my mind; it was a blank slate. As a teacher and speaker, I knew something was wrong. Filled with fear and desperation, I prayed, *Lord! Help me!*

When I finished praying that short, three-word prayer, I knew instantly what the problem was. I had begun that day saying to God, *"What You say, Lord, I will do."* Looking back, I could see how I'd been given several tests that morning—tests from God Himself. There was the test of wearing the purple hat even when I didn't want to, and the test of asking James to pray with me. There was the test of marching around the church with James in tow and doing it seven times, not just once. But when the next and hardest test came—the test of putting ALL of my schillings into the offering basket—I did not obey. I stuck with my own plan instead of going with His plan. I prayed, I listened, but I did not respond fully to God. I felt like a fool, lower than the lowest, totally in the pits.

I awkwardly stood on the platform, with everyone staring at me and waiting for me to say something. I knew that my lack of obedience had affected my ability to speak under God's blessing. Nothing came out of my mouth. I needed to make it right with God. So, right then, in my mind and heart, I confessed, *Forgive me, Lord! I am so sorry for not doing what You asked me to do. Help me to say and do what You want me to.* And with that, almost instantaneously, words began to pour out of me! They came so quickly I almost forgot to pause and wait while Catherine hurried to translate my phrases. I knew that I had to tell everyone who was there exactly what had just taken place.

With tears flowing down my face, I told them what had just happened. I explained that I had heard God's voice telling me to put all of my schillings in the offering basket, but I had held back. God had asked me to do something that didn't make any sense to me, something that I wouldn't ordinarily do. And I didn't do it. I confessed to them that I had not only stolen from God when I didn't give, I had stolen from them and their church. I told them that I had asked God for His forgiveness, and now I was asking for their forgiveness as well. Shouts of "Hallelujahs" and "Amens" echoed in the church as I spoke and as Catherine translated.

There was now a growing sense of boldness rising up inside of me. I knew that it was the power and presence of God. I paused, waiting for what God wanted me to say next. I only wanted to say the words that the Holy Spirit put into my heart and mind. Then I said, "I don't believe I'm the only one who has not given as God has asked." Catherine translated my words into Swahili, and the room suddenly became very quiet. The smiles left everyone's faces. I went on, "I'm not the only one who did not obey God when the offering basket went by." After pausing, I continued, "I'm not the only one who needs to make it right with the Lord."

That's when I did something I would never have dreamed of doing. A thought came into my mind, and I knew it was from God. I believed He was telling me to do something, and part of me was hesitant to do it. But, not wanting to fail another test, I was absolutely going to do it! I slowly took off my purple, sweat-stained hat, not even caring about my matted-down hair. At that moment, how I looked didn't matter at all. I walked across the platform to where Pastor Angelo sat. He stood up, and I handed him my hat. He looked a little confused, so I explained that this hat was to be like an offering basket. I walked Pastor Angelo over to the front of the altar, and had him extend my hat in front of him with his hands. Words poured out of me again as I explained that the hat was purple in color, representing the royalty of God. I said, "In just a few moments, I am going to do what God asked me to do and put all my schillings into the hat."

With Catherine still interpreting, I told them that I would need to pull out from under my shirt the belt that was holding all my money. Endeavoring to be modest, I turned my back to them. It took me a few minutes to pull out all my stacks of paper schillings. There was silence while everyone waited. I turned back around and walked over to Pastor Angelo. Then I placed all of my shillings into the purple hat.

Pastor Angelo holding Donna's hat as she speaks.

Walking back over to the lectern, I turned to 2 Timothy 2:21 in my Bible and read: *"Those who cleanse themselves ... will be instruments for noble purposes, made holy, useful to the Master and prepared to do any good work."* I had experienced that very cleansing and freedom in Jesus. God had helped me obey Him. What freedom I sensed! Confidently I said, "Jesus can make right the wrongs in your life. He can help you obey Him. Tell the Lord what you have done. He loves you. He hears you when you call out to Him. There is always forgiveness in Jesus." I could sense the power of God's Spirit sweeping over the people as they bowed their heads and prayed.

I went on and said, "Now that you have confessed your wrongs and lack of obedience to Him, I want you to know the Lord Jesus forgives you, just as He promises! But there are still those of you who did not put in the offering basket what God asked you to give. You held back. You need to make it right. You can get out of your seats right now. You can come up to the altar and put it into the purple hat, just as I did."

I picked up my Bible, slowly walked back down the steps, and sat in my chair, overcome by what God was doing. Pastor Angelo stood in front of the altar holding the purple hat, waiting as the Holy Spirit worked in the hearts of the people. He waited. It was quiet. I closed my eyes and prayed. In my heart I knew I had finally done what the Lord wanted me to do. I was covered with what I can only describe as an invisible blanket of peace. It was then that I realized why God had James and me walk and pray around the church seven times. He was breaking down barriers in my heart as well as in other people's hearts, so that we could respond to what He was saying.

Tears came streaming down my face when I opened my eyes and saw a long line of people waiting to go up to the altar. As people stepped forward, they tearfully put their offering into the purple hat, while others up in front were quietly confessing to the pastor and he was praying for them in their Swahili language. It went on for a very long time; the overflowing hat had to be emptied several times. I was overwhelmed at the magnitude of what God was doing and at the outpouring of forgiveness, grace and love in Christ. I thanked

Him for working in people's lives and giving them courage to step out in faith and receive the blessing that can only come from a clean, forgiven, and obedient heart.

Later on, after everyone had left, Kathy, Bob, and I sat with Catherine and Pastor Angelo in his office. We were all amazed at the tremendous moving of God's Holy Spirit. About two hundred people had come forward that morning to give back to the Lord. Pastor Angelo told us that the offering that was given would more than take care of the church's financial needs for at least an entire year. I was totally flabbergasted! He said they would now be able to do some things that they had been praying about doing for a very long time. He mentioned that even though many of the people in the church had the resources, they had been resistant to giving to God's work there. Of course, I had not known this; nor would I have ordinarily chosen to speak about money or giving. But God knew all of this and used me to deliver His message. I also knew that without a doubt, just as God was taking care of the church's needs there in Mombasa, He was more than able and would also take care of our financial needs for the rest of our time in Africa.

During the entire time Pastor Angelo was talking, I was quietly praying whether or not I should give my purple skirt and vest to Catherine. To do so seemed to make sense, but I kept hearing in my mind a clear *No. Wait. It's not the right time.* So, instead, I gave to Catherine a bag with several skirts. I told her what the Lord had led me to do with the skirts while I was in Africa and how He impressed me each day with what skirt to wear. I described to her how, as I prayed and waited on Him, the Holy Spirit always showed me to whom I should give a skirt. It was hard for me to explain it to her; nevertheless, I could see that she was getting it, and she was very excited. She quickly replied that she wanted to pray, wait, and listen for the Lord in the same way that I had done, and would do this with all the skirts I'd given to her. She could hardly wait to see how the Lord was going to work! Wow! Not only was God using the worn skirts I was wearing, now He would also be using the skirts I'd given to Catherine as she learned to pray, listen, and do what He asked her to do.

Catherine, still overwhelmed at the amazing work of God's Spirit.

Later that day, when I changed out of my purple skirt outfit, I felt as if God was telling me: *I will let you know when to give it away.* Something extraordinary had taken place that morning while I was wearing that beautiful purple outfit. Not only had I learned the blessing of what happens when you do what God asks you to do even though it doesn't make any sense at all, but hundreds of others also learned it as well. Ever so slowly I was beginning to see that there was a divine connection between the skirt I was impressed to wear each day and the sharing of the message He would give to me as I was wearing it. I somehow knew that this purple skirt would be going to someone very special.

In the days that followed, the Lord would never again let me wear that purple skirt and vest outfit. But, true to His prompting, the day finally came when He let me know that it was time to give it away. And what a surprise and blessing it would turn out to be!

If you want to pray, listen, and respond to God...
When God asks you to do something you wouldn't ordinarily do,
obey Him even when it doesn't make sense to you.

CHAPTER THREE - REFLECTION PAGES

"When God asks you to do something you wouldn't ordinarily do, obey Him even when it doesn't make sense to you."

PRAY AND LISTEN TO GOD AS YOU READ THESE WORDS FROM THE BIBLE

Isaiah 30:19–21

O people of Zion, who live in Jerusalem, you will weep no more. How gracious he will be when you cry for help! As soon as he hears, he will answer you. Although the LORD gives you the bread of adversity and the water of affliction, your teachers will be hidden no more, with your own eyes you will see them. Whether you turn to the right or to the left, your ears will hear a voice behind you, saying, "This is the way, walk in it."

Exodus 16:4

In this way I will test them and see whether they will follow my instructions.

1 Samuel 15:22

But Samuel replied: "Does the LORD delight in burnt offerings and sacrifices as much as in obeying the voice of the LORD? To obey is better than sacrifice, and to heed is better than the fat of rams."

Isaiah 55:8–9

"For my thoughts are not your thoughts, neither are your ways my ways," declares the LORD. "As the heavens are higher than the earth, so are my ways higher than your ways and my thoughts than your thoughts."

Jeremiah 42:3,6

Pray that the LORD your God will tell us where we should go and what we should do.... Whether it is favorable or unfavorable, we will obey the LORD our God, to whom we are sending you, so that it will go well with us for we will obey the LORD our God.

1 John 1:8–9
*If we claim to be without sin, we deceive ourselves and the truth
is not in us. If we confess our sins, he is faithful and just and
will forgive our sins and purify us from all unrighteousness.*

2 Corinthians 10:3–5
*For though we live in the world, we do not wage war as the
world does. The weapons we fight with are not the weapons of
the world. On the contrary, they have divine power to demolish
strongholds. We demolish arguments and every pretension
that sets itself up against the knowledge of God, and we take
captive every thought and make it obedient to Christ.*

QUESTIONS FOR REFLECTION AND DISCUSSION

1. What are some examples in the Bible of God asking people to do something they wouldn't ordinarily do?

2. Describe a time when God asked you to do something that didn't make sense to you, or that you ordinarily wouldn't have done. How did you respond?

3. Contrast the behavior of Sarah in Genesis 16:1–5 and in Genesis 18:10–15, and the behavior of Mary in Luke 1:26–38. How did their different responses result in different outcomes?

4. In this skirt story, what were the "tests" given to Donna and how did she handle them? What do you think was the spiritual "stronghold" that initially kept her from obeying God at the church in Mombassa?

5. What weapons do we have as followers of Jesus that can demolish the strongholds that keep us from obeying God when He asks us to do something?

6. In what ways do you see the promises of Psalm 32:1–7 manifested in this skirt story?

7. In what areas of your life is God currently asking you to obey Him even though it doesn't seem to make a lot of sense from a human perspective? Take time to talk with Him in prayer about these areas.

PRAYER OF RESPONSE

Heavenly Father, Thank you for loving me, accepting me, and not giving up on me—even when I do not listen to, and obey, Your voice. I don't want to be spiritually hard of hearing or resistant to You. Show me if there is any area in my life where I am ignoring Your voice and not walking in obedience to You. I am sorry for my sin and I surrender it all to You. Forgive me through Your Son, Jesus. Through His grace won for me on the cross, and through the power of the Holy Spirit living in me, enable me to resist the attacks of the enemy and demolish every stronghold that would keep me from responding in obedience to You. Help me to successfully pass through my times of testing, knowing that You walk with me every step of the way. Give me courage to obey You even if it means I need to step out of my comfort zone. Give me faith to leave the results in Your hands, and to rest in Your perfect and providing care. In Your Son's name I pray, Amen!

SKIRT STORY NUMBER THREE—
JEAN

———

If you want to pray, listen, and respond to God…
Spend time in God's Word, even when it
seems like you don't have the time.

I lay in bed emotionally and physically exhausted. Sleep did not come. It had been a spiritually full, rollercoaster-like day for me. I was still keyed up, and my adrenaline level was high. My mind was still in "recall" mode as I kept going over and over in my mind the things that had happened earlier that morning at Pastor Angelo's church in Mombasa. Looking back on it all, I recognized how the Lord had obviously broken through my stubborn will, changed me, forgave me, and led me during those hours. When I cried out to God for help in my desperation, He responded—in a big way! By His grace and power, He turned it into a teachable God-moment and used me to help others.

Now the Lord was helping me to look back at my lack of obedience with an understanding of how He brought good out of it as I confessed it to Him and to others right away. The congregation had witnessed the dramatic work of the Holy Spirit taking place in me as I stood silently up on the platform not able to say a single word. They didn't understand at first what was going on when they saw me struggling, but it slowly became obvious to them, unfolding right before their very eyes and registering in their hearts. When I explained to them exactly what I'd failed to do—not putting all my schillings in the offering basket as the Lord had directed me—I could sense God's Spirit convicting them as He had convicted me. As they called out to Him in prayer, the barriers that kept them from obeying God were broken. They, too, were changed. Receiving God's grace, forgiveness and power, they learned the blessing of obeying God in a brand-new way. It was overwhelming to me now just remembering the long line of people patiently waiting to give their offerings to the Lord. Scores of people from the congregation, including some of the visiting pastors, teachers, and leaders from the Bible conference, had been touched by God's Spirit and responded. Some of them lingered around afterwards, asking for prayer or just wanting to talk about what they had experienced. They had witnessed a divine moving of God's Spirit, and they were filled with amazement at what the Lord had done. It had been an incredible morning.

Then, as I lay in bed, something happened—almost as fast as turning on a light switch. My mind flipped to what I would call a "stinking thinking" mode. I was bombarded by fears and doubts: *What have you done? You gave away all your schillings. Are you crazy? Now you're stranded here. How can you travel? How will you pay for anything?* I knew it wasn't good for me to be caught up in these thoughts or to camp on them for any period of time. I needed to flip off that switch of negativity. Immediately, while lying there on my bed in the darkness, I stretched my arms and hands straight up into the air. I whispered, *"Lord, thank You for breaking my stubborn will today and for bringing good out of it all. Help me to seek You first always. Help me to listen to You. Help me to trust You above all else. Take away these thoughts of fear and doubt. I cast these thoughts on You. Enable me to set my mind on You and who You are. Help me to remember Your Word and Your promises to me. Please give me wisdom and guide me by Your Spirit. Give me Your peace that passes all my understanding."*

Then I began speaking out loud, not in whispers any more. I started saying bits and pieces of verses I'd memorized from the Bible and words from worship songs and hymns that I had sung over the years. I slowly felt the Holy Spirit move my mind from the negative to the positive, as words tumbled out of my mouth:

"Thank you Jesus. Thank you Lord!"
"God is my refuge and strength, a very present help in trouble."
"I cast my cares on You."
You are with me always."
"I have the mind of Christ."
"All things work together for good, according to Your purposes."
"I can do all things through Christ who gives me strength."
"Thou dost keep him in perfect peace whose mind is stayed on Thee."
"I am trusting Thee, Lord Jesus, trusting only Thee."
"All night. All day. Angels watching over me."

I actually started picturing angels around me as I continued saying out loud the things that God brought to my mind. I kept on thanking Him for His goodness to me and also for the many people who I knew were praying for me. Trusting in Him, I finally fell asleep, resting in His peace, not counting sheep but counting blessings.

Waking early Monday morning with the dull and haunting wail of the Muslim call to prayer, I was immediately pulled back into the reality of our situation and our desperate need for funds. I opened my thick and well-worn Bible, and some torn pages fell out. While picking them up, my thoughts drifted back to the day my husband had given me this Bible in April of 1979, on our first Easter together as husband and wife. I had originally planned on bringing my thinner, lighter-weight Bible with me to Africa. But the Lord was relentless, impressing me to pack this thicker Bible. So, after wasting far too much time arguing with Him about how heavy it would be to carry on such a long trip, I'd finally tucked it into my carry-on suitcase. Since then, this Bible had served as a daily reminder that my husband was praying for me. When he gave it to me, he had written a verse on one of its front pages: *"Let the Word of Christ dwell in you richly, as you teach and admonish one another in all wisdom...."* *(Colossians 3:16)* Certainly God's Word was dwelling in me, and was enabling me to teach God's truth in many contexts on this trip. I knew I was helpless on my own, but God was doing His work through me. As He had promised me back at Violet's house in Nyahururu, He was already giving me opportunities to "be the head and not the tail."

For years I had underlined verses in this Bible that were significant to me, and had written notes in its margins during sermons, Bible studies, and my own devotional times. These notations had often given me help and direction when I was called on to speak. Now, at this early morning hour, I propped up my flashlight to shine some light on these well-marked pages and prayed for God's Spirit to direct me in His Word. I was led to read the fourth chapter of the book of Philippians in the New Testament. As I was reading, I came across the words of Philippians 4:6–7: *"Do not be anxious about anything, but in everything, by prayer and petition, with thanksgiving, present your requests to God. And the peace of God, which transcends all understanding, will guard your hearts and your minds in Christ Jesus."*

Donna safely under a mosquito net.

God had clearly directed me to this book and this passage of the Bible! These words once again gave me His reassurance. I rejoiced in how relevant God's Word is, even though it was written centuries before. I kept on reading until God's Spirit stopped me on Philippians 4:19: *"And my God shall supply all your needs according to His riches in glory in Christ Jesus."* Wow! This Word from God was like a laser beam penetrating deep into my heart. God's Spirit was leading me and teaching me. Convicted of my worrying, I turned my fears and anxieties over to the Lord as I prayed, *"Thank you, Lord. You are much more capable than me."* Almost immediately I again experienced the peace He had given to me right before I had fallen asleep the evening before. I didn't know what we would do, but I did know that God would work things out and take care of all our needs as we looked to Him for direction. Right at that moment, I was actually excited and anticipating how the Lord would work it all out!

Now it was time for us to think about our next destination— Rwanda. Bob, Kathy, and I needed God's wisdom and direction since I had given away all my schillings. After taking time together in His Word and in prayer, we once again revised our itinerary and developed another scaled-down budget for the remainder of our time in Africa. The thought came that I should contact my husband in California. He was able to wire additional funds to us. Without question we knew the Lord had blessed my giving in Pastor Angelo's church the day before, and He would provide us with the financial support we needed for the rest of the trip. We also knew that He would take care of our itinerary. Later that evening, we would be leaving for the fifteen-hour-long bus trip back to Nairobi, arriving there on Tuesday morning. From Nairobi, we would fly on a small plane to Kigali, Rwanda, arriving Tuesday afternoon. I could hardly wrap my brain around all that traveling yet to come. But one thing for sure, the Lord had impressed in my mind over and over again: *I am with you. You will have all that you need, when you need it.* I was learning to lean on Him not only for financial needs but also for physical, spiritual, and emotional strength. This journey to Africa was turning out to be the most intense thing I'd ever done in my entire life.

Finally, after taking care of all our financial business and getting our luggage and containers organized and packed, we went out on the bamboo balcony to have one last little meal together in Mombasa. We pooled all our leftovers of bananas, mangos, papayas, and muffins. And, almost on cue, the little monkeys playfully scampered down from the branches of the trees, seeming to know that we were getting ready to leave. Although they were sometimes annoying and messy, they were fun to interact with. They teasingly scurried around, begging and squealing for some last bits of food. As we looked out through the trees to the ocean, the beautiful white sand beaches and clear blue skies of previous days were gone. They were replaced with cool gray skies, and low-lying, heavy-looking clouds; since it was low tide, the wet and gray-looking sand was now overtaken with piles of seaweed. A lot of trash was scattered all around, leftovers from the hordes of people who'd been there the day before. The beach was now devoid of tourists. It was as though the Lord was giving us a sign, through the dreariness of the weather and the condition of the beach, that it was time for us to move on. That's how the Lord works sometimes when you take the time to ask Him and then just stop, look, and listen. He will give you such signs and help you notice what is really going on around you.

Since we had some time before leaving for the bus station, we decided to take one more walk out on the almost-deserted beach of the Indian Ocean. The ominous clouds were piling up, and a light wind was beginning to blow. We playfully took off our shoes, squishing the cool, wet sand between our toes. Before long, the wind picked up and blew some of the sand into my sore eyes, which were still red and irritated from all the crying I had done the day before. I knew I needed to quickly go back to my room and wash the grains of sand out of my eyes.

As I was hurrying back to our bungalow, I kept hearing the loud voices of African men yelling back and forth to one another. I had not heard these kinds of sounds on any of the previous days we'd been there. It scared me, but I kept on going. Then, while looking up to my room as I approached the building, I saw the door swing open, and a tall, shirtless African man came out and ran quickly down the stairs. As he ran past me, I moved back. In his hand was a long and threatening-looking machete. Oh, my! I knew enough not to call out or ask what he had been doing up in my room. Feeling frightened, I went up the steps as fast as I could.

When I entered my room, I found the lock on my suitcase had been broken off. My stuff was scattered all around. Thank God I had taken time to put my valuables, including my passport and visa, into my belt underneath my shirt before going on our walk. All I could say was *"Thank you, Lord for protecting me!"* He had kept me from going into the room while the machete-wielding intruder was in there. Once again I heard God gently reminding me of Joshua 1:9: *"Do not be afraid … the Lord your God will be with you wherever you go."* I knew that the Lord was watching over me; now, more than ever, He was making it clear that this was no longer a safe place for us to be.

Shortly after that, we made it to the bus station and boarded our bus without any difficulty. It was a long and uncomfortable trip to Nairobi, accompanied by all that came with traveling by bus in Africa—frequent stops, getting on and off the bus, going through checkpoints, and trying to sleep through the loud music and sounds from everything around us. Upon our arrival in Nairobi, we were able to get a small van to take us and all our cargo to the airport. Exhausted, we boarded our plane for the five-hundred-mile flight west to Rwanda. I mistakenly thought, *I can finally get some sleep*, but it didn't happen. Strong, gusty winds and turbulence left us nauseous and numb. All of us were thankful when our plane landed safely in Kigali, Rwanda.

Pastor Moses, a wonderful Rwandan man with the most enormous smile, welcomed us. Still somewhat queasy from the flight and walking unsteadily, I was grateful when he gladly helped me with my luggage, got us through the security inspections, and helped us get our visas to enter Rwanda. Pastor Moses had arranged for several vehicles to transport us, our luggage, and all our containers. Soon we were on our way, traveling through the streets of the city.

Kigali is the capital of Rwanda, with a population of over one million people. Ringed by mountains, the city sprawls across four ridges with valleys in between. The vehicles took us up a winding hillside road to a gated mission house. Overlooking the beautiful flower-covered terraced hills of the city, this mission house accommodated large groups of people who were visiting from throughout the world. It was built around an inside courtyard, where much of the cooking was done for all the guests. Standing outside this mission house, I looked down from the top of the hill and could see locals everywhere along the streets selling their goods, including baskets of brightly colored fruits and vegetables. At that moment, I visibly understood why Rwanda is often called the "Garden Country" of Africa.

Pastor Moses had arranged for us, along with some of the other visitors who were staying at the mission house, to take a tour of the Kigali Genocide Memorial Center. We quickly unloaded our things into small, dorm-sized rooms. As I opened my suitcase to change out of my clothes, I prayed, *"Lord, what about my skirt—should I give it away today?"* No answer came. Long ago I had learned a phrase, "If in doubt, leave it out." So I knew it was not the right time. I quickly washed my face and headed out the door of my room to the front of the house. I didn't want to keep anyone waiting for me.

Moses gathered us in the courtyard, and we climbed into a modern-looking sightseeing van. Obviously this tour was a popular one, as hundreds of tourists were flocking to the country of Rwanda. While settling into our seats, we heard the crackling sound of a microphone, and the onboard tour guide began telling us about the horrific civil war that had taken place there eleven years before. We listened intently to him while trying to get accustomed to the cadence of his accent, which was different from a Kenyan accent. We didn't want to miss a word of what he was saying. What he began to tell us touched us very deeply.

Our guide told us that, prior to the civil war, 85 percent of the population of Rwanda was made up of Hutus, who were basically agriculturalists. The remaining 15 percent were a mixture of other minorities, mostly Tutsis. Being more educated, the Tutsis eventually took control of governing the country. Even though they were much smaller in number than the Hutus, the Tutsis slowly began to act in a racially superior way over the Hutus, even forcing many of them into slave labor. There was unbelievable tension and hostility between these two groups of people. It all came to a head in April of 1994, right in Kigali. Over the course of one hundred days—only three months—a civil war raged. There were mass killings of the Tutsis by the Hutus. Using mostly clubs and machetes, the Hutu militia violently stormed through the capital city, rampaging government offices and slaughtering the Tutsi civil servants who worked there. Then, with their evil hatred growing stronger and stronger, Hutus went onto the streets of Kigali and into Tutsi homes, murdering scores of families, including women, children, and even infants. As word of this spread quickly throughout the country, the Tutsis retaliated.

This only caused the violence against the Tutsis to escalate. Entire villages of Tutsi and Hutu people ran from their homes to escape. Parents hid children in the surrounding jungles. Others sought refuge in churches. Even in small towns and villages, Hutu militia forced the local Hutus to kill their own Tutsi neighbors, or face death for themselves and their families. In mixed marriages of Tutsi and Hutu, the Hutus were forced to kill members of their own families, or be killed. The Hutus even entered hospitals and killed off the injured survivors. Finally, with the intervention of United Nations forces, the unthinkable nightmare ended. During those one hundred days, almost one million Tutsis—75 percent of their population at the time—were killed; in addition, countless numbers of Hutus and other nationalities died. Twenty percent of the entire population of Rwanda lay dead. Another one million people saw their homes destroyed and became refugees. Now, a decade later, the nation was still trying to recover.

Upon arriving at the Memorial Center, we quietly exited the van and were taken to a garden where we saw two very long and wide mass graves. Tens of thousands were buried there. Surrounding the garden was a wall, inscribed with the names of many of the victims.

My mind had a hard time grasping the sheer totality of what I was seeing. The Memorial Center vividly told the story of the terrible genocide. We walked through room after room housing memorabilia and other historical valuables. Hundreds of tourists crammed into the unair-conditioned building and moved slowly through its dimly lit hallways, whispering in hushed tones. Suddenly, while I was peering through the glass at a display of numerous piles of human bones, my mind took me back to another time in my life. It was when I toured the Nazi Auschwitz-Birkenau concentration and extermination camp outside of Krakow, Poland. One out of every six Jews who died in the Holocaust had been murdered there. I couldn't help but reflect on what happens to people when that kind of sheer evil overtakes their minds and hearts.

At that moment, I felt sick to my stomach and overcome with sadness. I needed to get out of there, longing for fresh air. Somehow, through the maze of rooms and hallways, I made my way back to the outside, where I sat down on a bench, putting my head down. I was physically and emotionally spent. I needed time to process all I had heard and seen. When I looked up, Pastor Moses was standing there. He sat down beside me. I asked him how he had made it through all the violence and bloodshed of that horrible civil war. I was totally unprepared for what he shared, but I listened to his every word. Like water rushing out of a faucet, he began telling me his story.

Pastor Moses was a Hutu, and his wife, Rose, was a Tutsi; their children, of mixed ethnicity, were also considered to be Tutsi. As the orders to kill all Tutsis came down during those horrible three months, he—and his family, congregation, neighbors and friends—were forced to make incredible decisions. With tears running down his cheeks, he told me how he faced death himself because he, being a Hutu, would not slaughter his Tutsi family. Instead, he chose to hide them and lie about it to the Hutu militia.

I was shocked and stunned as I listened to Pastor Moses over the next two hours. In my whole life I'd never heard a story like his. I hung on his every word, learning how he and his family survived. Without a doubt, the Lord had protected them. It was almost like

Pastor Moses was preaching a sermon to me as he talked about God's great love and the tremendous sacrifice He made when He allowed His very own son, Jesus Christ, to come to the earth, to suffer, die, and rise again. Pastor Moses spoke about Jesus being a living example of God's saving love. He kept saying, *"Jesus did it all. Jesus did it all."* *"Still today,"* he said, *"we need the Lord."* The people of Rwanda were not only dealing with such overwhelming losses, they were also wrestling with how to forgive those who had done these horrifying things. Only God could intervene to truly bring about total love, forgiveness and reconciliation, so that the Hutus and Tutsis could live peaceably and coexist with their neighbors. This humble man knew that God had saved him for a reason. He wanted to be a "God example," showing his fellow Rwandans how to love and forgive others with the help of Christ.

Pastor Moses recounted story after story of the enormous struggles that had taken place, the unbelievably great pain he endured, and the huge personal losses he and others had suffered. Eleven years after the genocide, court trials were still taking place. People were being rounded up, arrested, and brought to trial for various crimes they had committed during the civil war. They were being held accountable for all that they had done. Pastor Moses told me that there were different kinds of trials. Those arrested for severe crimes, such as murder, were tried inside the courts. Those who were arrested for lesser atrocities were being tried in outdoor courts.

I noticed one of these outdoor trials taking place as we drove through the countryside on our way to the mission house. The people were sitting on long, narrow benches, facing a lectern where the accused stood. Over 120,000 trials like this were being held in local communities all over Rwanda. Those convicted of lesser crimes—such as robbery and destroying property—were not jailed, but sentenced to work in their communities for a given time period. They were identified by pink shirts that they were required to wear. Now I knew why I had seen so many people wearing pink shirts as we traveled through the streets of Kigali. Under the watchful eyes of armed guards, these pink-shirted people worked around the city restoring roads, reconstructing buildings and homes, and planting gardens to once again beautify the country of Rwanda. It was a small repayment for what they had done. I wanted to hear more but the tour was over, and it was time for Pastor Moses and me to return to the bus.

The ride back to the mission house was uncomfortably silent. We were all processing what we had seen and heard back at the Memorial Center. After getting off the bus, we headed over to the dining room. Surprisingly, there were around thirty guests ready for dinner. I was still reeling from being at the Memorial and wasn't hungry at all, but I knew it would be rude not to eat at least some of the food the lovely African women had prepared over the outside wood fires. They gave us plates on which was rice, green beans, and some kind of boiled, gray-looking meat. For dessert we had our choice from plates piled high with many different fresh-ripened fruits, recently harvested from gardens growing on the hillside around the mission house.

Since I wasn't very hungry I decided to move around the room, wanting to get to know some of the people. I asked them who they were, where they were from, why they were there, and how long they would stay. I sat down across from one middle-aged couple from America who had been coming to Rwanda since the genocide of the civil war. They had chosen to spend their vacation times helping wherever they were needed, both at the mission house and also in the orphanages around Kigali. Many children who had survived the genocide were left homeless after the civil war. Not only had these children lost their parents and their family and friends, but many of them had also suffered unbelievable pain and seen unspeakable things. Some had lost limbs; others had been mutilated or raped. This couple's eyes filled with tears as they told me how one little child's eyes had been poked out. Then they went on to tell me more incredible stories. I was touched to the core by this older couple's desire to do what they could to provide a safer and more comfortable place for these very young and homeless victims. It was obvious to me that they were not people of great means, but they were overflowing with love and generosity as they offered their skills, resources, and time to enable children in Rwanda to begin rebuilding their lives.

After praying for this couple, I got up and helped myself to a small banana. While I ate the banana and looked around the room, I prayed for God's Spirit to lead me to whomever He wanted. My eyes stopped on a middle-aged woman sitting by herself. Intuitively I knew she was the one the Lord wanted me to meet. I walked over to her table and asked if I could join her. Her name was Jean. I told her I could remember her name because "Jean" was my middle name. It's amazing how God works through little things like a name in order for us to make a connection with someone. Thinking she was visiting Rwanda on her vacation, I asked her how much time she had left before heading back to America. She laughed. And then, almost immediately, something deep inside of her seemed to open up. Leaning in closer to me, she looked deeply into my eyes and began to tell me her story. Her voice and demeanor changed as words came quickly from her. She was from the state of Washington where, until recently, she had lived her whole life. Although happily married to a wonderful husband, they were never able to have children. Then, quite unexpectedly, her husband became very seriously ill. They went through all the avenues of medical tests, surgeries and treatments, but without success. So they prayed and then decided to stop the treatments and leave it all in the Lord's hands. Although it was difficult, Jean faithfully cared for her husband at home with the help of friends. After many months, he died and was set free from all his pain and suffering.

When she finished her story, I reached over to take Jean's hand and comforted her. She grabbed me. I held her as she sobbed and sobbed for a long time. She was bottled up with pain. How good God was to guide me to her so that I could be a listening ear and simply love on her! Jean knew, without a doubt, that she would meet back up with her husband one day. And God knew exactly what she needed now—to share her pain with someone. Jean needed me, and I knew I needed her, too.

After we talked for a while, I asked Jean how she'd ended up there at the mission house. She told me that, back home in Washington, she had read an article about the living conditions of young women in

Rwanda. She learned that there were many women whose husbands had been killed in the genocide; others had lost their husbands to AIDS. Desperate to support their families, some of these young women were prostituting themselves in the streets. Jean couldn't stop thinking about what she had read in this article. As she prayed about it, she felt the Lord was leading her to travel to Kigali and see these things for herself. When she came, her heart was so touched by what she saw that she returned to Washington and sold her house and most of her earthly possessions. Then, since she had no family or ties there, she moved to Rwanda.

Shortly after she arrived, Jean began walking through the streets of Kigali. As she did this, she started getting acquainted with the women who were involved in prostitution. You simply have to picture in your mind's eye this sweet, middle-aged, gray-haired American woman walking the streets of this African city. Would these young women really listen to her? Some didn't, but many did! Jean told them that there were other ways to support themselves. Those who were willing to leave their life of prostitution she trained with new skills or helped find a job. She told me how she taught some of them business skills, even supporting some financially until they could make it on their own. Her eyes danced as she recounted stories of young girls whose lives had been changed. What excited her the most was that she had been able to tell them about Jesus. He was the One who had led her to leave her home country to move to Rwanda and to live simply so that she could help others simply live. Long after everyone had cleared out of the dining room, Jean and I were still talking. But my eyes were heavy, ready for much needed sleep. After praying together, we hugged each other goodnight. We both knew that the Lord had given us the precious blessing of our time together. We had been strangers, but now we were sisters!

I don't think I even changed out of my clothes that night as I climbed into my bed. I laid my backpack on the bed and pulled out my flashlight, Bible, and journal for the next morning. Wrapping the mosquito netting around me, I felt my body sink into the thin mattress. I missed my husband and my comfortable home, but I knew

I couldn't think about that now. Not only was I fatigued from the fifteen-hour overnight bus trip from Mombasa, I was also emotionally undone; I was still overwhelmed with all the horrible brutality I'd heard about that day. It grieved me so much. I prayed, *"Help me, dear Lord."* Exhaustion set in, and sleep quickly came.

The low and deep sound of the Muslim horn woke me the next morning. Hearing voices and unfamiliar sounds, I sat up on my knees and looked through the bars of the open window. I could barely see a faint light in the sky. Out in the courtyard the Rwandan women were already up, placing wood in the pits to start fires in order to boil water. Over and over again I was humbled at seeing how hard and selflessly people worked. Life there was demanding and harsh, yet these women were happy to have a place to live, food to eat, and work to do.

Curiously, I selfishly started thinking about the possibility of getting some coffee. Oh, my ... coffee could be a real possibility! Coffee!! Coffee!! Since this was a mission house that hosted many American visitors, they just might have some coffee for breakfast. Then I became ashamed of myself for thinking about my own selfish wants.

Pastor Moses, along with his wife, would be arriving later that morning to accompany us to Gisenyi, Rwanda. There, we would be hosting a leadership conference for pastors and their wives who were coming from neighboring Congo and Rwandan villages. Since we would be returning to the mission house later in the week, I needed to sort through my bags and repack only what would be essential for the next several days. I had a lot to do in a short period of time. *"Show me what to do."* I prayed, *"Help me to slow down and focus."*

There I sat in the early morning darkness, on my little twin-sized bed, wrapped in a mosquito net. All I knew was that I needed God's help and direction. I quietly said to Him, *"I don't know what to do, but my eyes are on you."* Then, the song "Open My Eyes, Lord, I Want to See Jesus" started coming to my mind over and over again. So I said, *"I need to see you, Lord. Open my heart to know what to do this day. Should I give my skirt away? Whom should I give it to?"* The clock was ticking. I kept waiting. I kept praying. *"Yikes, Lord," I said, "I have things to do! Quiet my mind. Help me to focus on You."* I waited some more. And, just like that, the name "Matthew" popped into my mind. *"Okay! Direction! Thank you, Lord!"* Propping up my flashlight against my backpack, I flipped open my Bible to Matthew, the first book of the New Testament. Turning through the pages, I stopped in chapter 25. I read through the verses of the chapter, praying the Lord would teach me what He wanted me to learn. After I read verses 40 through 46, I stopped. *"What are you telling me with these verses?"* I asked the Lord. I pondered the words of Jesus in verse 40: *"I tell you the truth, whatever you did for one of the least of these brothers of mine, you did for me."*

With these words, my mind drifted back to the people I had met the night before in the simple little dining room. They were ordinary hardworking people who were giving of themselves to make a difference in the lives of the "least of these" here in Rwanda. I thought of the couple who had researched how they could make a difference after the genocide. They asked God for help and guidance. Then, they acted. Instead of going on a cruise, they decided to use their funds to come here instead. They had become difference-makers. And, they had been coming here ever since.

As so often happens when I take the time to read God's Word, the Lord was putting things into my mind. In conversation with God, I said, *"I want to be like them. I want to make a difference. I want to live out this passage in my life for You. I want to live more simply, so that others can simply live. Help me, Lord, to do that. Show me what to do and how to do it."* I kept reading these verses in Matthew over and over again, listening for what He wanted to say to me. I knew that the Holy Spirit had stopped me in this chapter, and that He had something to teach me.

That's when a face appeared in my mind. It was the face of Jean, the widowed lady I'd met the night before. She had sold everything to move here from America, leaving the comfortable and familiar behind so that she could answer God's call to help young women on the streets. She was living out these words of Jesus in Matthew 25.

That's when I knew who the recipient of my next skirt would be. Jean! Jean, of course! I laughed with joy at the way God was working.

At the moment I knew that I would give Jean a skirt, I also knew I was to give her several more of the skirts that belonged to Barbara. Barbara was a widow and, like Jean, she had given up most of her worldly goods, including her home. She, too, was devoted to going wherever the Lord would take her. This was another one of those "God connections" that He so often shows us when we take time to pray and listen to Him! The Holy Spirit also brought to my mind the other items my sisters and other people had given me. I knew now why I had not been led to give them away before now. I had things like little purses, pretty necklaces, bracelets, some perfumes, soaps, and other brand-new toiletries. Jean could give these to the young women she was helping on the streets. They liked things like that; sometimes they even sold themselves so they could purchase them. Receiving these things from Jean might even encourage them to leave behind what they were doing.

With that, I finished my prayers and closed my Bible. Even though I didn't think I had time to spend in the Word that morning, God had helped me to take the time. Now He gave me enough time to once again put on my sister's skirt and to sort my things into one bag. I prepared a container and set it aside to give to Jean. With Bible in hand, I headed off to the dining room. I didn't find any coffee. *Bummer!* I thought. Oh, well, I was a woman on a mission—a mission to find Jean. I stepped outside into the courtyard and almost walked right into a little African woman who was bent over sweeping the sidewalk with a broom tied together with twigs. I introduced myself and learned her name was Florence. I asked her if she knew where I could find Jean. She led me around the courtyard and pointed to Jean's room.

I knocked on the door. Surprised to see me, Jean welcomed me in. Her room was very small, with only a bed to sit on. She invited me to sit down. After I sat, I told her that the Lord had given me a message, and I needed to talk with her about it. I showed her in my Bible the verses in Matthew 25 the Lord had led me to that morning.

I told her how, as I prayed, the Lord had brought her face into my mind. I asked her how I could pray for her. Jean shared some of her struggles, fears, and needs; she talked about how lonely it was for her to be so far away from her church and friends, even though she knew this was exactly where God wanted her to be. She needed someone to listen to her, to encourage her, to hug her, and to pray for her. God knew this, and He put the thought into my mind to go and talk with her. We had a priceless time of prayer together.

I then asked Jean if she could come back to my room with me, as the Lord had impressed it on my heart to give her some things. When we got to my room, I told her what I was doing with skirts that had been given to me from women in America. I shared with her how I was led, that morning, to give her several of my friend Barbara's skirts. I told her how much she and Barbara were alike in many ways. For some reason, I had also been prompted to give her a set of brand-new sheets that Barbara left with me. And then suddenly, Jean began to cry. Through her tears, I learned she had been wanting some pretty sheets for her bed, but she didn't want to spend money on herself to purchase any. She felt that would be selfish. I, too, shed some tears! Rather than just leaving the sheets back at Violet's house in Nyahururu, I'd been led to hold onto them and carry them around for days. I had met many deserving people who could have used those sheets, but the Lord had me save them for this very moment. They were for Jean, the one who needed them the most. When I gave her the other things to give away to the young women, along with some toys for little children and Bibles inscribed from friends in America, you would have thought I'd given her thousands of dollars. We hugged each other tightly, knowing that the Lord had brought all this about.

Seeing through the open door of my room that the bus had arrived, I quickly grabbed my stuff and headed out to the court-yard. After one last hug with my new friend, I climbed on board. As the bus rolled away, I looked back and saw Jean standing there on the roadway, still waving. I had experienced the joy and blessing of meeting a fellow "sister" in the Lord, and now I was feeling the pain of leaving her. But I was also experiencing over and over again the intimate sense of God's presence. Sitting in the bus, I quietly pondered all that had happened to me here in Kigali, and I prayed, *"Thank You for leading me to Jean. Please watch over her, help her and bless her. Thank You for helping me to take the time to be in Your Word, and for making me attune to Your Word by reading it, waiting for You to lead me, and then taking action when You speak. Forgive me, Lord, when I don't take the time to do this but instead do things my own way. I want to follow Your leading, not my own thoughts. Thank You for showing me more and more of You. Help me to always be willing to wait and listen to Your voice. I love you so much. Thanks for loving me, too. Amen!"*

If you want to pray, listen, and respond to God...
Spend time in God's Word, even when it seems like
you don't have the time.

Jean with her brand-new sheets.

CHAPTER FOUR - REFLECTION PAGES

"Spend time in God's Word, even when it seems like you don't have the time."

PRAY AND LISTEN TO GOD AS YOU READ THESE WORDS FROM THE BIBLE

Joshua 1:8–9

Do not let this Book of the Law depart from your mouth; meditate on it day and night, so that you may be careful to do everything written in it. Then you will be prosperous and successful. Have I not commanded you? Be strong and courageous. Do not be terrified; do not be discouraged, for the LORD your God will be with you wherever you go.

Colossians 3:16

Let the word of Christ dwell in you richly as you teach and admonish one another with all wisdom, and as you sing psalms, hymns and spiritual songs with gratitude in your hearts to God.

Psalm 1:1–3

Blessed is the man who does not walk in the counsel of the wicked or stand in the way of sinners or sit in the seat of mockers. But his delight is in the law of the LORD, and on his law he meditates day and night. He is like a tree planted by streams of water, which yields its fruit in season and whose leaf does not wither. Whatever he does prospers.

Acts 17:11

Now the Bereans were of more noble character than the Thessalonians, for they received the message with great eagerness and examined the Scriptures daily to see if what Paul said was true.

2 Timothy 3:17

All Scripture is God-breathed and useful for teaching, rebuking, correcting and training in righteousness, so that the man of God may be thoroughly equipped for every good work.

Romans 15:4
*For everything that was written in the past was
written to teach us, so that through endurance and
encouragement of the Scriptures we might have hope.*

Matthew 6:33
*But seek first his kingdom and his righteousness, and
all these things will be given to you as well.*

QUESTIONS FOR REFLECTION AND DISCUSSION

1. What do you think it would be like to live in a nation that had gone through what the people of Rwanda experienced?

2. Read Psalm 19:7–14 in your Bible. What does this psalm say can be the blessings of spending time in God's Word even in the most stressful and difficult times of life?

3. Where in this skirt story did you see spending time in God's Word made a difference in Donna's life and in the lives of others, and what was the difference it made?

4. What did you learn about servanthood from Jean's life?

5. How does spending time in God's Word help you to be a better servant who is equipped for every good work?

6. Imagine a Christian friend saying to you, "I just don't have time to read the Bible every day." How might you respond?

7. What action, if any, do you want to prayerfully take after reading this skirt story about Jean?

PRAYER OF RESPONSE

Lord, I don't know where I would be without You and Your Word in my life. You are my Lamp, and the unfolding of Your words shows me what to do and the way I should go. I not only want to hear You in Your Word, I also want to live out what You say to me—I want to grow in praying, listening, and responding to You! Help me to be consistent in reading my Bible every day—even in the most difficult of times. Holy Spirit, I know that You work through Your Word to grow my faith. Give me increased faith to take consistent time in Your Word, even when it seems like I don't have the time. Thank You for helping me to see a bigger picture of servanthood. As I spend time in Your Word, equip me to live a life of compassionate and loving service, trusting in You to meet all of my needs. In turn, may I be Your healing hands in this broken and hurting world. In Jesus' name I pray. Amen!

SKIRT STORY NUMBER FOUR— ROSE

If you want to pray, listen, and respond to God…
Devote yourself to a life of prayer, depending upon God
to work out the details.

Our bus pulled out through the front gates of the mission house and headed down the hill. I watched until I could no longer see Jean waving her hands as she stood in the roadway. Still consumed with my thoughts about how the Lord had connected us the night before, I thanked Him for giving us time together and for the way His Spirit led me to give Barbara's sheets, along with her skirts, to Jean. I reflected on how much the Lord cares about us—even when it comes to the seemingly ordinary things of life—and how He used me to be a blessing to Jean. Praying for her, I said in my heart, *Lord, give Jean special joy today. Encourage her heart through all that just happened, especially in the way You granted her desire for some new sheets. Give her new strength. Open new doors of opportunity for her to help women on the streets. Thank You for working out this connection in Your mighty name, Amen!* No doubt God had done a huge thing in both of us, drawing us closer to Him and also to one another.

Looking out of the front windows of the bus, I saw a sign saying, "Gisenyi." That was where we were headed, off on yet another adventure.

Pastor Moses had arranged transportation with a tour bus company, which meant we would not have to make any stops at periodic checkpoints, bus stations, or for people waving their hands for us to pick them up. Even then, it would take us three to four hours to travel to Gisenyi, where we would be staying for two nights in a small local motel. It was close to the border city of Goma, Congo. We would be going there the next morning. Goma, a city of approximately one million people, rests on the shore of beautiful Lake Kivu. It sits only 8 miles south of the crater of an active volcano named Nyiragongo. This volcano had erupted only two years before and destroyed over 40 percent of the homes and buildings in Goma. Now volcanic activity was once again threatening the city. To get to Goma from our motel in Gisenyi, we would walk a long distance to the Congo border, get passes at a guarded checkpoint, and then walk across a dangerous and unguarded "No Man's Land" between Rwanda and the Congo. We definitely needed God's help and protection with all that was still ahead of us.

Kathy, who had been seated in the back of the bus, made her way up to the front where I was sitting. She told me that a pastor in Goma, Pastor Donat, had invited her and Bob to speak the next morning at his church. Many community leaders were going to be present for the rededication of the church, which had been destroyed and then rebuilt following the volcanic eruption two years before. What a wonderful opportunity!

After Kathy returned to her seat, I quietly prayed for the Lord to use me in whatever capacity He wanted. I just wanted to be available to serve Him. I would need physical strength to do all the walking that was ahead, especially on the uneven, lava-ridden roadways taking us through dangerous territory. On top of that, being a foreigner in the Congo meant there was always a target on our backs. *Prepare the way, Lord.* I pleaded in my heart, *I truly want to be used by you. And show me what to do with my skirt.*

As we got closer to Gisenyi, we passed through a volcanic region. Columns of smoke were actually coming out of several of the live volcanoes. It was a spectacular, though threatening, sight. While it was beautiful, part of me wanted to get away from there as quickly as possible. Yet I also knew I was where God wanted me to be.

The next two days were an incredible time for me. I saw God work on our behalf in many ways. Continuing to wear my sister Jan's skirt each day, I could sense God's strength and protection covering me in response to her prayers. I was privileged to speak at Pastor Donat's church in Goma, Congo. I also had the opportunity to share, and pray, with other pastors and their wives at the leadership conference in Gisenyi. My eyes still tear up as I remember the humble pastors and their wives who came to that conference. They were serving and ministering to many displaced and hurting people. We were able to give them school and medical supplies, along with prayer shawls for the ladies; we also gave the pastors recordings of some of my husband's sermons, along with small players and batteries. And, even though I prayed about giving away my skirts—especially the purple one—the Lord was silent about doing so. Seeing many opportunities to give the skirts away, part of me wanted to follow my own instincts but I didn't. I didn't know the reasons for waiting yet I held back, looking for God's promptings and choosing to listen to Him rather than to my own human nature.

Playing drums in the newly rebuilt church in the Congo.

When Friday morning arrived, it was time for us to leave Gisenyi and head back down the mountains to the mission house in Kigali. In the beautiful outdoor gardens of the local motel where we stayed, we ate a lovely farewell breakfast with lots of fresh fruit, entertained by a chatty African grey parrot caged nearby. We also had a wonderful time of sharing and prayer with all the pastors and their wives. After many hugs, we said our final goodbyes, loaded our bags back onto the bus, and were on our way.

Upon arriving back at the mission house in Kigali, Kathy and I took time to repack the containers and all our bags. Although we were tired, we knew we wouldn't have time to do it the next morning since we'd be leaving very early to go to the bus station. Because it was a fifteen-hour ride to our destination in Kampala, Uganda, we wanted to get to the bus station early in order to purchase tickets for a more comfortable bus. It would be nice to be able to travel with fewer noisy animals—like goats, chickens, and dogs—on board with us. But our early morning departure meant for a very short night.

The following morning, awakened by the 4:00 a.m. call to prayer, I looked outside through the bars of my window with my flashlight. In the darkness, I could see that it was raining. No fires were burning this morning. Grabbing my Bible, I knew I needed a word from the Lord. Remembering that a good friend was praying through Psalm 91 for me each day, I turned to that passage and read these words: *"He who dwells in the shelter of the Most High will rest in the shadow of the Almighty. I will say of the LORD, 'He is my refuge and my fortress, my God, in whom I trust.' Surely he will save you from the fowler's snare and from the deadly pestilence. He will cover you with his feathers, and under his winds you will find refuge ... He will command his angels concerning you, to guard you in all your ways."* (Psalm 91:1–4,11) Then I talked to the Lord in prayer: *"Lord, traveling by bus isn't easy; but traveling in the rain with all these containers is really hard and also dangerous. Help me to rise above all these difficulties and struggles. Send your angels to guard and protect us. Be my umbrella and shelter, and shield me from danger. Keep my thoughts centered on you."*

A minivan arrived to take us, our baggage, and the rest of our containers to the bus station. The rain was still pouring down when we arrived. Crowds of men, women and children, with all kinds of animals as well, were hurrying to get their tickets. There was so much confusion, and no one to help us. Not only that: as I looked around, I could see that all the signs were written only in Swahili. I sighed and prayed, *"Lord, where do we go? Which bus should we be on? How can we possibly do this? What if we somehow miscommunicate to the ticket person and get on the wrong bus to the wrong place?"* I suddenly felt a pain in the pit of my stomach. I knew it was fear. Anxiety was building up inside me, and too many thoughts were colliding around in my mind. I kept praying. *"Help us, Lord! Show us what to do. Send your angels to watch over us."*

As we struggled to unload all our stuff, we were bombarded with men who came over to "help" us for only a few schillings. We knew better than to accept their offers. Some of them were just trying to get work, but we'd been told to watch out for those who would take everything you had and run away with it. As traveling Americans, we were their prime targets. Stopping at an open area between some of the busses, Kathy and Bob told me to wait right there and keep an eye on all of our things while they went inside to get the tickets. As they hurried away, I thought to myself: *What? Guard all of this stuff, in this chaos?* I stood there in the rain, my hair dripping wet, loaded down with my backpack and trying to keep my carry-on bag steady in the thick, gooey red mud. I was also guarding Bob and Kathy's bags and all of our containers as well.

Cold, wet, miserable and now alone, I looked at the men hovering around me. Some of them were very tall—well, I guess all of them were taller than me! And some of them were big and stocky; they were all staring at me. I knew they could very easily knock me down, and in nothing flat, take off with everything. I needed to look like a Goliath! So I prayed, *"Lord, help me to look huge, like a Goliath! Put a hedge of protection around me! Thank You for Your umbrella of peace in this storm."*

It seemed like an eternity until Kathy and Bob reappeared. After much negotiating and a "tip" to the ticket agent, they got the last three seats on board the more comfortable bus. All I could say was, *"Yea! Thank you, Lord!"* We somehow managed to shove our bags and containers into the storage compartment of the bus, praying, *"Lord, keep all of these things safe, all the way to Kampala!"* Climbing on board with our backpacks and carry-ons in tow, we moved cautiously down the slick and muddy aisle, looking for vacant seats. Thankfully, Kathy and I found two seats side by side, and Bob found one at the very back.

Getting myself situated on the sticky vinyl seat, I looked out the window, waiting and wondering what was taking so long for our bus to leave. After a while, several armed soldiers came on board and asked three passengers for their passports and all of their papers. Those three passengers were Bob, Kathy, and me. The soldiers confiscated our passports and papers and left. Bob followed quickly behind them. Now we were learning more about what it really means to *"pray continually."* (1 Thessalonians 5:7) Kathy and I prayed and prayed! I remembered the words, *"We do not know what to do, but our eyes are upon You."* (2 Chronicles 20:12) Waiting in God's presence, when we were totally helpless to do anything but pray, was building our faith. The time passed ever so slowly. We kept praying. It seemed to take forever. Finally, Bob climbed back onto the bus carrying all our passports and paperwork. I thought, *Thank you, Jesus!* At that moment, I was reminded how important it was for us to continually focus on God's protection and provision in order to get us safely through each and every situation. He was our shelter and shield, and would be faithful to honor His promise in Joshua 1:9: *"For the LORD your God will be with you wherever you go."*

Finally, with the rumbling sound of the motor and the screeching of the gears, we were on our way to Kampala. Because of the bus continually lurching from side to side, and the loud, thumping music being played over the intercom, it was almost impossible to converse with anyone, let alone sleep. So I looked out the window, taking in the beauty of the Rwandan countryside. Along the way, in small towns and villages, I saw more community trials taking place with all the accused standing up front in their pink shirts. I also saw many people who had been maimed during the massacre begging by the side of the road. They were balancing on stumps for legs, crying out for help. Some had no hands; others had arms or legs missing. As I watched them, my mind went back to a young orphaned girl I'd met two nights before in Gisenyi. Her whole family had been killed during that horrible genocide. She was the only survivor. Incredible as it sounds, even though she was an infant, her eyes had been gouged out. Miraculously, she had survived. I'll never forget the look on her face as she sang about Jesus, the God who loved her and saved her. Then my thoughts went back to the older couple at the Mission House in Gigali who had chosen to give up so much in order to make a difference in the lives of orphaned children. I asked the Lord to bless them in what they were doing.

Sitting there on the bus, I remembered how—when Jesus walked along the roads—people cried out to Him for help. My heart stirred inside of me. I, too, wanted to help them all. But, it just wasn't possible. There was so much pain, so much poverty, so much illness, so much sadness and death. I fervently prayed, *"Lord, it's all too much to take in. What can I do? Please show me. Help me not to forget. Help me to live more simply so that I can help others to simply live."*

Our bus finally stopped at the border between Rwanda and Uganda, along with at least a dozen other busses. Everyone had to exit all the busses and walk from one country to the next. However, the three of us were once again singled out and separated from the crowds. Accompanied by armed guards, we were escorted down a long path and into a guardhouse. It was quite scary and intimidating as we filled out additional forms, paid a fee, and waited for our passports and papers to be returned to us. The guards firmly questioned each of us individually, asking why we desired entry into their country. The family right ahead of us were not allowed to go through. I just kept praying. The worship song, "God Will Make a Way" came into my mind, and I asked God to go before us, making a way through this checkpoint. I remembered Brother Andrew who was called "God's Smuggler." He had smuggled thousands of Bibles into countries behind the Iron Curtain in order to give them away to people who needed God's Word. The Lord made the border guards blind to all of the Bibles he had packed into his little car. I prayed the same would happen for us as it happened for Brother Andrew. Joshua 1:9 again came into my mind. *"Do not be afraid ... for the LORD your God will be with you wherever you go."*

Finally we got everything processed and found our way back to the bus, grateful that our young driver had not left us behind. Although I was still feeling cold and damp from the rain, I was thankful to the Lord for being our shield and protector. He was watching over us and had gotten us through yet another obstacle. With miles to go, it was a very long time before we finally arrived on Saturday evening at the bus station in Kampala, Uganda.

We were greeted with great big smiles and hugs from two local pastors—Pastor Steve and yet another Pastor Moses. It had become obvious to me that Moses is a popular name in Africa. Having already arranged transportation for us, these two pastors helped load all our bags and containers into a minibus. My head was still ringing not only from the loud music we had endured for the past 15 hours, but also from the chatter of people in a filled-to-capacity bus, as well as from some noisy animals we had picked up along the way. The air in Kampala was hot and heavy, a sharp contrast to the cool mountain air of Rwanda. My tongue stuck to the roof of my mouth, for I had long ago finished off the last of my bottled water. Grateful for the quiet of the smaller bus, I sat gazing through the windows at the city of Kampala. Kampala is the capital city of Uganda and borders Lake Victoria, which is Africa's largest lake. I was surprised to see how modern the tall buildings were in and around the city, more so than in any of the previous capitals we'd visited.

After about 45 minutes, we turned off the main road onto a narrow, deeply rutted and dusty street on the outskirts of Kampala. In the early dusk of the evening, the driver maneuvered more slowly, weaving his way around barefooted, naked children who were running and playing in the streets. From my vantage point on the small bus, I could see women sitting by open fires outside little huts, cooking some kind of food in sizzling pans of grease. Pastor Moses had arranged for us to stay in a safe and secure house on this dusty street. The house was the home of a prominent colonel in the Ugandan military. The colonel's wife, Rose, was a Christian and had been a faithful member of Pastor Moses' church for years. The driver pulled up to a large red iron gate, where guards with semiautomatic weapons appeared. Already, a small crowd of onlookers from the surrounding neighborhood started to gather around our bus. Pastor Moses hopped out and began speaking to the guards in Swahili; within minutes, the heavy gates opened. The driver drove slowly into the front courtyard of the colonel's compound, stopped the bus, and opened its doors.

As we stepped down from the bus, people of all ages poured out of the house. Many children swarmed around us, excited and eager to help us unload all our things. Kathy was grabbed by a very robust, jolly-looking African woman. It was the colonel's wife, Rose. Rose then got a hold of me, hugging and squeezing me very hard. She led us inside, taking us through a maze of dimly lit rooms that made up the main house. I would be staying in a bedroom inside this large house.

Rose then took us to an enclosed courtyard outside the back of the house. She told us that over fifty people lived in this compound. Standing there, I observed high walls all around, with shards of broken glass cemented into the tops of the walls. Along the entire left side of the courtyard were small rooms to accommodate the soldiers who guarded the colonel and his family. Along the back and right sides of the courtyard were tiny rooms, each large enough for only a small bed or mattress on the floor. These rooms housed the many children running around the compound. The colonel and Rose had only three children of their own, but they had rescued a large number of orphaned children from off the streets; many of these orphans has lost their parents because of AIDS. It was becoming apparent to me that Rose and the colonel had mighty big hearts. Rose then pointed out one of the rooms that had a door; this was where Kathy and Bob would be staying. She also walked us over to a room that had a pipe coming out of the ground with cold water dripping from it. This was the room where we could shower.

Off the courtyard there was a large room. This room was used as a kitchen for the preparation of each day's meals. It took a lot of effort to prepare food for everyone who lived in the compound, including the soldiers. I looked inside this kitchen and saw young girls giggling together as they cleaned and cut up vegetables. A few older girls were putting a mound of something purple inside banana leaves, wrapping each one carefully and then boiling them in pots over several open fire pits. Running around in the courtyard were lots of chickens. Not only did these chickens supply eggs for the many people living there, but I also learned later that several of them would become our evening meal.

In another part of the courtyard, I could see children washing clothes in tubs and hanging them on lines to dry. After showing us around, Rose led us back into the main house where she gave us a much needed glass of water.

Pastor Moses was waiting in the house to take Kathy, Bob, and me to his radio station in Kampala. We were scheduled to speak on his church's hour-long radio program both on Saturday night and again on Sunday morning. I needed to quickly freshen up as best I could. On my way back to the room where I'd be bunking with several African girls, I peeked inside of a somewhat larger room with its door slightly ajar. In this room I saw a single lit candle somehow anchored on the cement floor. A number of children were sprawled around this candle on thin mats, lying on their bellies and writing in spiral notebooks. I also spotted a couple of younger children sorting through a big pile of rice, licking their fingers and picking out little bugs. They told me it was the rice they'd be cooking us for dinner. I thought, *Oh, my! Too much information!* and shot up a quick prayer, *Lord, help me not to think about that right now.*

I hurriedly changed out of my damp clothes and went out the door with Pastor Moses, Kathy, and Bob to a waiting taxi. The sky was now pitch-black. Occasional glimmers of light from fires and from candles inside of open huts pierced the darkness. We were squeezed together, bumping into each other, as the driver steered around ruts and holes in the darkness. I suddenly felt very fatigued and drowsy in the warmth of the taxi. Before long, we pulled up to Pastor Moses' radio station. It looked like a very small house. Inside was equipment that had been purchased with donations from Christians in America.

Pastor Moses had us sit around a small desk, giving each of us a microphone. Once we were on the air, he invited us to briefly tell about ourselves and why we had come to Uganda. When it was my turn I said a quick prayer, asking the Holy Spirit to tell me what to say. As I spoke, I was humbled that God was giving me yet another opportunity to witness for Him as He put His words into my mind and out my mouth. After each one of us shared, Pastor Moses invited people to call in with their questions for us to answer. Many of the people calling in said they wanted to talk to "the woman with the small voice." Sitting there in that tiny radio station, broadcasting to the more than one million residents of Kampala, I was overwhelmed at the goodness and faithfulness of the Lord. He was fulfilling my childhood dream and the desires of my heart in yet another unbelievable way!

Donna broadcasting on the radio in Uganda.

When we arrived back at Rose's house later that night, we were surprised to find that her husband, the colonel, was also there. Although this was Kathy's seventh and Bob's second visit to Rose's house, they told me they had never met the colonel; he had always been away on military matters. But now, for the very first time, he was home. I thought to myself, *Hmmm. This is no coincidence!* Compared to Rose, the colonel was small in size and stature but charismatic and welcoming. He kept asking us question after question about where we had been and where we were going. We told him of our desire to take food and clothing, as well as medical and school supplies, into the refugee camps outside of Gulu, Uganda. We weren't sure if this would even be feasible because of war-torn conditions in that area, as well as the presence of rebels from the Sudan who were attacking people in and around the camps. The colonel seemed very interested in helping us, giving us information and telling us story after story of the things that were happening in his country.

As we sat at the table talking, each one of us took turns eating, because they had only a few plates. When one was finished eating, the plate would be rinsed off for the next person. There were no eating utensils; we used our fingers to eat what was served. I noticed that the children were quietly waiting for the adults to finish so they could finally get their turn to eat whatever was left of the food. Although I was intrigued with all of the colonel's stories, I was ready to find my bed and get some much-needed sleep. After I said my "thanks" and "goodnights" to everyone, Rose led me down a dark hallway with a candle. She planted this candle on a small bench under the window by tipping it and then sitting it down on the drips of hot wax to hold it in place. Although the house was wired for electricity, it didn't necessarily mean that it was always available. The local government had the authority to turn it on and off. And tonight, even in the colonel's house, it was off. Rose turned back towards me, smiled, squeezed me once again with one of her giant hugs, and left. She seemed to know, at that moment, how very much I needed a special human touch.

After doing a quick wash and brushing my teeth using my bottled water, I crawled into bed and placed the mosquito netting around me. As I laid my head down on the thin mattress and flat pillow, I prayed, *"Lord, quiet my heart. Help me to sleep."* I kept saying little bits and pieces of God's Word as they came to mind until I finally fell asleep.

I awoke early the next morning to the now familiar sound of the horn. So as not to disturb the six girls all piled together on two small bunk beds, I gathered my things and quietly slipped out of the room. I tiptoed back to the front room of the house. There I found Rose kneeling on the floor by a yellow flowered-fabric sofa, praying. She got up smiling, unmistakably eager to talk with me. Rose motioned for me to come over and sit down at the table since both of us had heavy Bibles in hand. I asked her how long she'd been a Christian. It was like floodgates opening as words came flowing out of her. She gave me a condensed version of the amazing transformation that had taken place in her life when, as a Muslim, she met Jesus Christ many years before. Her face was aglow as she talked about the day of her baptism and described how Jesus had washed away her sins. She shared how her faith in Christ was still growing each day. Opening her well-worn Bible, she showed me some of her favorite verses; I was blessed by her obvious knowledge of God's Word and her desire to teach it to her own children as well as the rescued orphans she and the colonel had brought to live with them in their house.

I asked Rose how I could pray for her. She told me the colonel was a very good man but he was not a Christian. So, there in that candlelit room, we held hands and prayed together for the colonel to say "yes" to Jesus knocking on the door of his heart. I was blown away by the intensity of Rose's prayers—this woman knew how to pray! Assuring her that God would honor the prayers of her heart, I shared a Bible verse with her that was very dear to me: *"Delight yourself in the LORD and He will give you the desires of your heart."* *(Psalm 37:4)* We hugged each other, thanking the Lord we had this early and undisturbed time together—a time that allowed us to get to know one another at a deeper level. As I headed back to my room, I silently asked, *"Is Rose to get a skirt, Lord?"*

I walked back into my dimly lit room and got dressed. The night before, Pastor Moses had asked me to teach Sunday school that morning, so I needed to get my objects together before he would arrive to take us back to the radio station. While rummaging through my bag, my hand touched one of Barbara's skirts. At that moment, I knew it was the exact skirt I would give to Rose! Wow! I whispered, *"Thank you, Lord, for such a quick answer!"*

Stepping outside the front door onto the porch of the house, I was startled to find the colonel sitting there with several other military officers. I apologized for disturbing them and went down the steps. I knelt over, scooped up some red dirt, turned and headed back toward the house. As my eyes became more accustomed to the streaks of light in the morning sky, I could see they were watching me, curious why I was digging and gathering dirt. I stepped back onto the porch and stopped to explain that I needed the dirt to use in a talk I was giving in Sunday School that morning. Then, hardly without taking a breath, I asked, "Are you coming to church?" Even as the words rolled out of my mouth, I was thinking, *I can't believe I just said that!* The colonel was very nice but answered that they were going into the city for an important meeting and wouldn't be able to make it. I respectfully replied, "Oh, I understand." Then, without hesitation, I asked, "May I pray for you?" The officers looked at me with startled expressions on their faces. The colonel said, "Yes, please." As he started to get up, all the rest of them stood—many of them still holding their semiautomatic guns. I began to pray. I prayed for God's guidance upon the decisions they were making, for wisdom they needed because of the warfare that was going on in Uganda, and for personal help and safety for them and their families. Certainly God had prompted me to do this and gave me the words to pray. In the years since then I have often thought of that moment, and am still amazed that I—a short little woman with no earthly author- ity—had the boldness to do such a thing. But I'm confident that the devotional and prayer time I had spent with Rose helped me to step out in faith and boldness. And, as a result of this encounter, the Lord opened a door that would prove to be a life-saving moment in the journey that was ahead of us.

The hours that followed that early Sunday morning encounter with Rose and the colonel were memorable ones. Bob, Kathy, and I had another opportunity to speak on the radio, with many people phoning in and responding to the messages we shared. Later on we saw God's Spirit move powerfully during Sunday School and in the morning worship service at church. The church was simply a large tent in a slumlike neighborhood, complete with mooing cows and crowing roosters. But the Lord was truly inhabiting the praises of His people in that church! After lunch, I had a wonderful opportunity to spend some time sharing with the young women who were my roommates back at the colonel and Rose's house. Before I knew it, it was time for us to return to the church for their evening worship service.

Rose, along with all the children living in the compound, walked with us back to the tent church. Since I had been invited to speak that night at the service, I'd been praying throughout the afternoon, asking God to show me what I should share. But nothing came. I had learned to simply keep waiting and praying at times like this. I walked into the tent, found my seat, sat down with my bag, and continued to pray. I had heard that marriage problems were very prominent in Ugandan society, so the thought came into my mind to tell the church about my husband and share with them what we had learned about building a strong marriage relationship with the help of the Lord.

When it was time for me to share, I felt the Holy Spirit nudging me to talk about the fact that—early on in our relationship, even before we were married—we would read the Bible and pray together, and that we'd continued doing this ever since. I explained, "Honestly, I don't remember most of those prayers or even the answers to them. But what I do know is that, as we prayed, our hearts were being knitted together. Ecclesiastes 4:12 says, *'A cord of three strands is not easily broken.'* Jesus is that third strand, and with every prayer we prayed, He began to bind us closer and closer to Him and to each other. We didn't do it perfectly, but we did it; even when we didn't feel like it, we prayed. We've talked to the Lord about all kinds of things—our jobs, our children, family problems, ear infections, chicken pox, stitches, broken down vehicles, the death of parents, family and friends. We've prayed for people who needed God's love and healing from debilitating diseases. We've thanked Him daily for being our Lord and Savior, for providing food, clothing, and other things for us. We've asked for wisdom and help in making decisions about many things. Countless times we've prayed, '*We do not know what to do, but our eyes are upon you.*' (2 Chronicles 20:12) We've also heard each other praying, 'Lord, I'm sorry for what I said and did to my spouse. Please forgive me.' Sometimes we've prayed aloud just riding in our car or walking. Other times we've held hands and prayed silently when we were too overwhelmed for words, as when we held our infant son moments after he died in the hospital. Praying like this throughout the years has created a strong connection between us that is not easily broken. Over and over again we have seen God work in our lives and in the lives of our family and friends. But we know that we aren't finished yet. We are still asking the Lord to teach us to pray and to keep us praying with and for each other, because we know that '*The prayer of a righteous man is powerful and effective.*'" (James 5:16)

Then, while holding back tears, I told them how—before I left home to come to Africa—my husband had taken time to write down thirty different notes to me. He put them in separate envelopes so I would have a note to open and read every day I'd be gone. I held up the stacks of envelopes so that they could see them. I went on to explain that each note contained sweet words of care and love from my husband, a word of Scripture, a prayer, or sometimes a verse from a song or a hymn. These loving and beautiful notes had encouraged me and carried me through some very tough days on this trip. Up until now in these notes, my husband had not asked me to do anything. But in today's note, he asked me if I would sing a hymn—a hymn about prayer—right there on the continent of Africa. It was his late father's favorite hymn: "What a Friend We Have in Jesus." I asked if anyone knew the song. To my amazement, hands shot up in the air along with many loud "A-mens!" Then, in broken English, with no instruments playing, we sang together these beautiful words:

What a Friend we have in Jesus, all our sins and griefs to bear!
What a privilege to carry everything to God in prayer!
Oh, what peace we often forfeit, Oh, what needless pain we bear,
All because we do not carry everything to God in prayer!

When we finished singing and I said, "Let's pray," I was surprised when people spontaneously began getting out of their seats and coming forward for prayer. God's Spirit worked again and again that evening, as many individuals and couples came for prayer, seeking healing for their marriages. Jesus also brought physical healing of all kinds to many people. I was deeply touched by how many people desired to make a change in their marriage and to commit themselves to pray with and for each other. What we saw that night was a living testimony to the power and effectiveness of prayer!

Afterwards, while walking back in the darkness to the colonel's house, I felt a little scared. I could sense people were watching us, and I was glad there was such a large group of us. Upon our arrival, the colonel was waiting for us. I could see by the look on his face that he was excited about something. During his meeting in the city that day, he'd seen a friend of his who was a major general in the Ugandan military. The colonel told him of our desire to take food and supplies into the refugee camp outside of Gulu. After hearing this, the major general said he wanted to have a meeting with us the very next day. I thought, *Lord, you got us an appointment with a major general? This is amazing!* God was surely opening doors for us as we prayerfully put the desires of our hearts before Him!

The next morning, I awoke full of excitement and thanks to the Lord for all He had done the day before. I prayed, *"Lord, what shall I wear today?"* It was my sister's skirt again! I knew she would be praying for us even though she had no idea of our meeting with the major general later that day. Pastor Moses arrived with a taxi to accompany us into the city. We needed to do lots of errands in town prior to our meeting with the general. We knew we had to hurry; being late for a meeting with a major general was absolutely not an option!

Upon our arrival at the hotel where our meeting was to be held, we immediately saw a number of armed guards standing by a covered patio. We concluded that was where we were to go. Pastor Moses went ahead of us and spoke a few words in Swahili to the guards. Then we were all escorted to a table at the far end of the patio. As we approached, the major general stood up dressed in his impressive military uniform. He was a tall, physically fit man, exuding strength and authority. He tilted his head forward and bowed as he shook our hands. Even though we were in the company of such a high-ranking officer, I immediately felt at ease, responding to his kind and gentle nature. After a while, his wife and son joined us for a late lunch. As we all ate, the major general began asking us many questions. We talked about our desire to go into the refugee camps to teach God's Word, to pray for the refugees, and to bless them with food and supplies. We shared with him that it was our prayer that we could give the refugees hope for their future, tell them that God has a plan for them and assure them that people had not forgotten them—just as God had not forgotten them. The major general listened intently and asked still more questions. We had hoped to have at least thirty minutes or so with this very important official but, surprisingly, our meeting lasted for more than three hours! It was clear that God was giving us great favor with him.

After we answered all of his questions, the major general's heart was so moved with compassion that he did something truly extraordinary: on the spot he gave us—for however long we would need it—his very own personal double-cab truck, which was heavily armored with extra bumper bars in front and back, complete with darkened windows. He also said that he was immediately assigning to us his personal driver, along with an armed guard who would provide us protection at all times. And the general didn't stop there. He gave us the name of the commander of the Ugandan military base in Gulu. When we arrived there, we were to contact this commander. He would give us all the necessary clearances and would also provide additional guards for our protection when we traveled into the refugee camps.

With that amazing answer to prayer, I hopped right out of my chair, went around to the head of table, and stood next to the major general and his family. I asked him if I could lay my hands on them and pray for them. I told him that I knew he needed prayer for the enormous decisions he faced each day, for his desire to do what was good and right for the people of Africa, for his safety, his family's safety, and for the Lord's favor and blessing on them all. He replied that he and his family were Christians, and they welcomed prayer. So I prayed! When I finished he stood up, thanked me, bent over, and gave me a hug. We took a few pictures, and then he motioned for his guards to come over. He spoke quietly to them for a few minutes.

After we said our thanks and goodbyes, the guards led us over to the major general's truck parked out on the street. From that moment on for the rest of our time in Uganda we had his truck, his driver, and his armed escort. No longer would we have to wait for a bus or have to pay for taxis wherever we went. God had shown Himself to be a God who *is able to do immeasurably more than all we ask or imagine, according to His power that is at work within us.* (Ephesians 3:20)

After meeting the major general's driver, Henry, and the armed guard, we all climbed into the highly polished, sparkling clean, sapphire-blue truck. It was a thing of beauty! Had not the Lord said to me, *"You will have all that you need when you need it?"* Wow! Not only were we given a spacious truck to carry us and all of our things to the refugee camps, we also had a driver and an armed guard! Knowing that we could never thank the Lord enough for what He had done for us, I quietly prayed, *"Thank you, Jesus, for moving the major general's heart to bless us with what we need to accomplish our work in the days ahead. Bless him and his precious family. I give You all glory and honor for what You are doing here."*

Pastor Moses didn't have to give Henry directions to the colonel's house as he already knew the way. I couldn't help but notice people staring at us as we drove through the streets of Kampala. Other vehicles seemed to move out of the way, recognizing the presence of an important governmental vehicle coming through, possibly carrying a great dignitary. As I have since thought about that, I realize that we were not "nobodies" but were really "somebodies." We were children of King Jesus—the greatest dignitary of all! He was demonstrating His protective power and love for us in this most incredible way!

I was glad when we finally pulled into the front courtyard of the colonel's house. After the heavy gates slammed shut, we climbed out of the truck. Rose came rushing out of the house. She gave me the most enormous and tight hug, and I realized how happy I was to see her shining face! I rejoiced that God had given me a new friend and thanked Him for allowing me to meet this awesome woman of prayer. I knew that her prayers for us were making a mighty difference during our time in Uganda. Rose wanted to hear all about what happened and how we ended up with the major general's personal truck, his driver, and guard. When we told her, she jumped up and started shouting "Hallelujah! Thank you, Jesus!"

As the day wore on, my body was more and more fatigued. I knew I needed time alone to get ready to leave for Gulu early the next morning. I found Rose and explained to her my need to stay home instead of going to the tent church that evening. After everyone left, I found myself writing little notes to give to all the young women in my room and also to the orphaned children. My daughter, Kristin, having spent the previous summer in Africa, told me that Africans love to receive pictures, especially pictures of family. So I had brought along many copies of a picture of my husband, Kristin, and me. On the back of these pictures, I spent time writing a special Bible verse for each person. I had just finished writing on the last picture when everyone returned from church.

Rose called all of us to come to the front room of the house where I saw the colonel sitting as well. She had anchored several candles on the cement floor. We all sat down on the floor circling the candles. A couple of the children—Julia and Jovia—had written a song for me. The day before, I had taught a song to these two little sisters who had been rescued by the colonel from the streets of Uganda. They had written the words of the song that I taught them in their little spiral notebooks and also made up another verse just for me. It was hard to hold back the tears as these little orphan girls sang the words of their special love gift. After many others shared their love and their stories, I pulled out the family pictures I'd written on and passed them out around the circle. The little children ran and hugged me, shouting with joy and delight at receiving such a simple gift.

Last of all, I pulled a very colorful skirt out of a plastic grocery bag. I explained to everyone how women in America had chosen skirts from their closets for me to give as the Lord directed. Pinned inside of this skirt was a note telling me that it had belonged to a powerfully strong prayer warrior back in America. I explained how the Lord impressed me to give this skirt to Rose, to encourage her as she prayed fervently each day. Surely her prayers were not in vain— what happened to us that day testified to the power and effectiveness of her prayers. Just like that, Rose jumped up and out of her chair, letting out the most enormous African squeal. She grabbed me and led me in dancing around the room with her and all the children as they shouted and gave praise to God. It had been quite a day!

Rose sitting in the courtyard, preparing the evening meal.

I awoke at the usual time early Tuesday morning. As I was praying, I sensed the Lord say to me, *I want you to give away that brand-new Bible.* Weeks earlier, before leaving America, I had been led to purchase a new Bible with gold pages. It was still in its original box in my suitcase. Even though I had asked the Lord many times about what I should do with it, I had not been impressed to give it to anyone until now. So I prayed, *Who's it for?* I heard in my heart, *It's for the Colonel.* I now had my marching orders. I got up and found the Bible in my bag. I knew I needed to write a message on one of its front pages before giving it to him. I prayed, *"Give me the words, Lord."* As the words came, I wrote a note to the colonel along with a Scripture verse. After dressing quickly, I went looking for him.

I found the colonel sitting on the front porch in the early morning darkness all by himself. I thought, *"Thank you, Lord!"* and stepped out onto the porch. I said to the colonel, "I have something to tell you." I then shared with him how God led me to buy this Bible and bring it all the way to Africa, and that I hadn't been led to give it to anyone until that very morning. I told the colonel that the Lord had impressed me to give it to him. I showed him what I had written in the front of the Bible: *"Believe in the Lord Jesus, and you will be saved."* (Acts 16:31) Holding the Bible in his hands, the colonel began to weep. I quietly told him that I knew God was calling him and preparing his heart to receive Jesus as His Savior. I explained how we are all separated from God by our sin, and how Jesus took our sins—and the sins of the whole world—upon Himself on the cross. When Jesus suffered and died there, He was separated from the Heavenly Father for all of us in our place, so that all our sins could be forgiven and we could live forever in Heaven with Him. Jesus was buried in the grave, but He rose again and ascended into Heaven, where He is now, preparing a place for all those who believe in Him. When we trust in Him as our Savior, we become adopted children of God, part of His Family forever!

Then it happened: right on the front porch of the colonel's home, with the first rays of morning light in the sky, I was totally humbled and privileged to lead him in a prayer. One phrase at a time as he repeated words after me, he asked Jesus to be his Savior and committed his life to Christ. We both hugged and cried. It was a "Hallelujah" moment, and the angels were rejoicing for sure! Just as we finished praying, Rose came out through the door, stepping on the porch. She knew something was up. After I told her what had just happened she squealed, and now all three of us were crying tears of joy. Rose had seen the answer to her persistent prayers—prayers she had prayed for many, many years!

A short while later, Rose and I prayed together a prayer of thanksgiving for what God had done. Surely we had seen again the importance of praying each and every day, and not giving up, but waiting for the Lord to do His work. Huddled in the corner of the kitchen, we praised God for the chain of divinely orchestrated events we had witnessed over the past three days. When we finished praying, I hurried back to my room and got my bags ready, for we had a long day of travel ahead of us to get to the refugee camps in Gulu. Before long, Kathy, Bob and I, along with Pastor Moses, had loaded everything into the major general's truck. We stood in a big circle in the courtyard, along with Rose, the children, Henry and the two armed guards, and said a prayer. No doubt God's hand had been all over our time there, working out every detail in our lives as we turned everything over to Him. He had brought us to this nation, in His time, and for His purposes and blessing.

If you want to pray, listen, and respond to God…
Devote yourself to a life of prayer, depending
upon God to work out the details.

CHAPTER FIVE - REFLECTION PAGES

"Devote yourself to a life of prayer, depending on God to work out the details."

PRAY AND LISTEN TO GOD AS YOU READ THESE WORDS FROM THE BIBLE

Psalm 88:1–2
O LORD, the God who saves me, day and night I cry out before you. May my prayer come before you; turn your ear to my cry.

Psalm 119:147–148
I rise before dawn and cry for help; I have put my hope in your word. My eyes stay open through the watches of the night, that I may meditate on your promises.

Romans 12:11–12
Never be lacking in zeal, but keep your spiritual fervor, serving the Lord. Be joyful in hope, patient in affliction, faithful in prayer.

Hebrews 4:14–16
Therefore, since we have a great high priest who has gone through the heavens, Jesus the Son of God, let us hold firmly to the faith we profess. For we do not have a high priest who is unable to sympathize with our weaknesses, but we have one who has been tempted in every way, just as we are—yet was without sin. Let us then approach the throne of grace with confidence, so that we may receive mercy and find grace to help us in our time of need.

John 5:17
Jesus said to them, "My Father is always at his work to this very day, and I, too, am working."

Proverbs 31:10–12
A wife of noble character who can find? She is worth far more than rubies. Her husband has full confidence in her and lacks nothing of value. She brings him good, not harm, all the days of her life.

Lamentations 2:19a
Arise, cry out in the night, as watches of the night begin; pour
out your heart like water in the presence of the Lord. Lift
up your hands to him for the lives of your children ...

QUESTIONS FOR REFLECTION AND DISCUSSION

1. If someone asked you, "What is prayer?" how would you answer them?

2. What does the story of the Canaanite woman in Matthew 15:21–28 have to say about faith, humility, and tenacity when it comes to your prayers?

3. In what ways were Donna and others blessed by her boldness in stopping and praying for the colonel and the soldiers?

4. Read Luke 10:38–42 in your Bible. How was Rose like Mary? Was Rose like Martha, too? Where do you find yourself in the Mary and Martha story?

5. What does this skirt story teach you about the place God wants prayer to have in families—including your family?

6. Describe a time when you prayed and depended on God to work out the details. What did you learn from that experience?

7. After reading this skirt story, what changes do you desire to see in your personal prayer life?

PRAYER OF RESPONSE

Jesus, I worship You for being the eternal Son of God who understands my every weakness. Because of what You did for me, I can approach Your throne with confidence and receive mercy and grace to help me in my time of need. Please give to me faith, humility, and tenacity like the

Canaanite woman, and help me to come to You with wild abandonment. In my private life may I be like Mary, sitting at Your feet and prayerfully listening to You. In my public life, grant me courage and boldness to step out and pray aloud with people in their time of need. Right now I pray by name for people in my family who need to know You.... Do in their lives what You did in the colonel's life! I give every detail of my life to You. I know that You, Your Heavenly Father, and the Holy Spirit are always at work in and around me, so I devote myself to a life of prayer, depending on You to work out all the details. In Your name of grace and power I pray. Amen!

SKIRT STORY NUMBER FIVE— MERCY

If you want to pray, listen, and respond to God…
Commit yourself to be sacrificially generous with God
and with others.

While still standing in our prayer circle at the colonel and Rose's house in Kampala, and before getting into the truck to leave for the refugee camps in Gulu, I looked intently at the faces of everyone around me. When I got to Mercy, I stopped. Her head was down. I knew she was overcome with emotion, probably thinking about all that had happened over the past few days. My mind drifted back to the day we arrived in Kampala and when we first met....

On the evening of that day, Rose gave us a tour of their heavily guarded home, taking us into a large, walled-in courtyard in the back of the house. An entourage of children surrounded us as we moved through the courtyard. While Rose was showing us around, I had an enormous, almost overwhelming feeling of anticipation that something was about to happen. I called out to the Lord in my mind. *Show me. Impress me with what this is all about.* I kept praying, shooting up what I call "arrow prayers" aimed right at the throne of Heaven. I recognized that this was not an ordinary thing going on inside of me.

Following Rose back into the house, my eyes slowly became accustomed to the dimness inside. That's when I saw her. Standing in the corner of the kitchen was a pretty young woman. She looked to be in her early to mid twenties. I stuck out my hand and said, "Hi! My name is Donna." She smiled, shaking my hand, and quietly replied, "My name is Mercy." As she spoke, something stirred inside of me. *What's going on?* I asked the Lord, even as I was shaking her hand. Then the words came into my mind, *"It's her! She's the one!"* I instantly knew what that meant. It was the answer to something I had been praying about every single day since my second week in Africa. I had been continually asking the Lord, "Who should get the purple skirt?" Now I had my answer. Mercy was the one to receive the beautiful purple skirt and vest outfit I'd worn on that miraculous day when God's Spirit led me to give away all my schillings at Pastor Angelo and Caroline's church in Mombassa.

Although I was totally excited, I wanted to make sure I'd heard from the Lord correctly. *Okay, Lord, why should this shy, timid young woman be the one to have the honor of receiving this skirt? Who is she? What is her story?* I knew I needed more information. I also knew I needed to pray for confirmation about this "word" from the Lord. Then my eyes focused back on Rose as she led us into the dining room, where she gave each of us a much-needed glass of water.

Because Moses was waiting to take us to the radio station, I had to change out of my musty-smelling clothes and quickly freshened up. Mercy led me down a hallway, stopping to show me the room that held the inside toilet. There was also a sink in the small room, but because there were no pipes to carry the water away, a bucket had to be put under the sink so the water wouldn't run down the drain and splash all over the floor. Mercy and I walked further down the hallway and entered a small bedroom in the back of the house. Surveying the room, I saw a narrow table against the far wall, one full-sized bed with mosquito netting, and a set of bunk beds—with one bunk bed stacked on top of the other. Mercy pointed out the full-sized bed, saying that it was the one I would use. The other six young women who slept there, including Mercy, would be sharing the set of bunk beds. That's right—there would be three young women, all of whom were larger-sized than me, in each of the twin-sized beds. I felt badly about having the larger bed, but I knew that this was their way of honoring and welcoming me. I noticed that under the set of bunk beds were small suitcases. I later learned that the young women kept all their earthly possessions inside those suitcases. Standing there with Mercy, I felt so humbled. As I continued to look around, I saw two windows in the room. These windows had no glass in them, but only iron bars going up and down. Pungent smells permeated the room from burning fires outside the surrounding homes and from sewage running down the sides of the street.

Some of the young women appeared, carrying my bags into the room. Rose also came in with a candle, so we could all see a little better. Then everyone left. I opened my bag, sliding my fingers over the purple skirt, now feeling very confident and at peace that the Lord was finally allowing me to give away this beautiful skirt. Changing quickly, I locked up my bag and headed out the door to go to the radio station.

Upon our return later that evening, we met the colonel, listened to his incredible stories, and took turns eating dinner. Soon it was time for me to head off to bed. I stopped by the tiny bathroom that Mercy had shown me earlier. Remembering to grab a bucket for the drain under the sink in the bathroom, I washed up, thinking about how much I was looking forward to a real shower after I returned home. When I got back to my room, I found all six of the young women—including Mercy—ready for bed. There they sat smiling, all squeezed together, with their legs dangling over the edges of their small beds. Although I was exhausted from such a long day, it was clear to me that they wanted to talk. *Oh, no!* I thought, *I am live bait! It's gonna be like a slumber party!* The writing was on the wall. I knew I didn't have the strength to stay awake, but again I remembered God's words to me, *You will have all you need, when you need it.* I definitely didn't want to pass up this opportunity for whatever the Lord wanted to do. I had already asked him for some kind of confirmation, or a sign, about the word He had spoken to my heart concerning Mercy. This could well be it. So I prayed, *"Okay, Lord. I need You! Give me*

Your strength and guidance. Keep my eyes open and my mind attentive for this special time."

Because of the open windows, mosquitoes were buzzing all around me; fearing I'd be bit, and not wanting to get malaria, I quickly put away my toiletries and my clothes. I grabbed my Bible and my backpack and crawled into bed. Mercy jumped up, along with some of the other young women. They lovingly tucked the mosquito netting in all around me. Then they all sat down on the bed. In a way, I mused, I must look like I was the captured "main attraction." But that was entirely fine with me! I found out each of their names, amazed at how well some of them spoke English. I wanted to know all about them, and they wanted to know all about me, including what it was like for me when I was a child growing up in America.

Earlier that evening, I had observed some of them cutting off the heads of chickens, scalding and plucking off their feathers, and then prepping them for cooking. It was something they did almost daily for meals. They were surprised to learn I had grown up on a farm in Texas where I, too, had cut off many a chicken head. I had learned to butcher hogs for meat, planted and harvested fruits and vegetables, and even picked cotton in hot fields while barefooted. The Lord kept bringing these things into my mind to tell them. I could see how God was using our similar experiences as a bridge to connect us to one other, while all the time building trust between us so we could talk about even deeper things.

They were listening closely as I told them about my husband and our daughter, who was in college. She was about the same age as most of them. I shared how I'd gone to college and became a teacher. I showed them a picture of my family; one of them immediately reached under the net, grabbed it out of my hands, and taped on the wall by the door. They, in turn, told me about their lives—how many of them had seen their parents slowly die from AIDS, and how each one of them had been rescued and supported by the colonel and Rose.

They wanted to know how I ended up coming to Africa. I recounted to them my childhood story of listening to missionaries who had come, year after year, to my church in Texas. I described to them my dream—my longing to teach in Africa—that began to grow in my heart. I told them about the stirring I felt throughout my life every time I heard or saw something about Africa. I explained how I had put that dream on a back burner of my mind, thinking that it could never really happen, and continued on with my life as usual. Then suddenly an opportunity came along, and God fulfilled my dream in a most unexpected way.

They leaned in with their eyes wide open as I told them about Barbara, my friend from my church in America. I related to them the story of her telling me that she was going to Africa to speak, and how—after days of praying—she offered to pay my way to come along with her, so that I could pray for her as she spoke. The girls wondered where Barbara was, and they were shocked when I told them Barbara's mother had died and that she had returned to America after only three days in Africa. I opened my Bible and showed them the verse God had given to me before I left my home. *"Have I not commanded you? Be strong and courageous. Do not be terrified; do not be discouraged, for the LORD your God, will be with you wherever you go." (Joshua 1:9)*

I went on to describe to them the many ways God had brought good out of the difficult circumstance of Barbara's sudden departure, including fulfilling my dream of teaching in Africa. I shared with them that after she left, I felt very lonely and confused, but God was with me and helped me through every day. That popped open even more questions and conversation about feeling alone, without any family. They certainly could relate to those feelings. I told them that when I woke up each morning, I would try not to think about my loneliness or sadness, but I'd purposefully think about the Lord. I would read my Bible and pray, and then I'd listen for what God wanted to say to me. I'd write down ideas in my notebook or journal as thoughts came into my mind; then, I'd pray some more and wait quietly on Him to help me.

Still sitting on the bed, the young women kept asking me questions. I could see that God was giving me another opportunity to teach in a most unexpected venue here in Africa. They asked me if

I was scared when Barbara left. "Yes," I said, "I was absolutely scared." But I told them that God kept bringing to my mind things He had taught me, songs or Bible verses I'd memorized, or stories I'd read in the Bible—even stories in the Scripture I'd heard as a child. Not only that, when I was asked to speak in place of Barbara at churches, orphanages, and other settings, the Lord would put ideas into my mind to talk about.

They immediately wanted to know how I knew it was God speaking to me. I paused, and prayed, *Whoa, Lord! Is this a wide open door for me, or what?* In my fatigued state I asked Him for help. *Lord, I'm so tired. But I can tell that this is the time. I need You to do this in me, and through me. You alone are my strength. Empower me by Your Spirit. Give me Your direction in this. I need clarity.* And clarity is just what the Holy Spirit gave to me. He led me to tell these six young women that if they truly wanted to hear from God and know His voice, they first needed to know Jesus by putting their trust in Him and what He had done for them.

So, at that late hour of the night, I began sharing with them the good news of Jesus! As I started to speak, I quietly prayed, *Lord, give me a simple illustration.* I knew they needed something tangible, something real that they could relate to. And into my mind came a picture of dinner plates, the dinner plates we had just taken turns eating from. I opened my mouth, and words like these began to come ...

"Do you remember when we all ate dinner tonight? After someone finished eating, the plate would be rinsed off, so the next person could have a clean plate to eat from. Surely, no one would want to eat from a dirty plate. Compare that to our lives. Because we sin, our lives are like those dirty plates. Try to imagine all the bad things you have ever done. Picture those bad things piling up on the dirty 'plates' of your heart."

"Although God loves us, He hates the bad things that we do, say or think. He calls these things sin. This sin separates us from our loving Heavenly Father and keeps us from life with Him today and living forever with Him in Heaven. It takes one, only one, of these bad things to do that. The Bible says, *'For the wages of sin is death....'* (Romans 6:23) A 'wage' is what you earn, what you deserve. And death is what we deserve from God because of our sin. Can you see the problem we all have, myself included? Yes, we have all sinned and are all guilty. Each one of us is guilty of not just one sin, but many, many sins."

"God is loving, but God is also just. Think about when people are found guilty and stand before a judge in a court of law. For justice to be done, they have to be punished for the bad thing they did. One day when we die, each one of us will end up standing before God, the ultimate Judge. We will certainly be found guilty of our sins, and will deserve to be punished for them. That punishment is death and eternal separation from God. That's why the Bible says, *'The soul who sins is the one who will die.'* (Ezekiel 18:20) Can you see that? We all need help. Our plates—our souls—are dirty. We have sinned, and we are guilty."

As I spoke these convicting words, I could tell that these six young women were tracking along with what I was saying. *Thank you, Lord,* I prayed in my mind, and then continued....

"Way back in the very beginning, after God created all things, He made a man named Adam and a woman named Eve. He also made a beautiful garden for them, the Garden of Eden. God had a wonderful relationship with Adam and Eve. He loved them, and they loved Him. But, one day, they ate the fruit from the tree of the knowledge of good and evil, even though God had commanded them not to do it. He said, *'When you eat of it you will surely die.'* (Genesis 2:17) After they had eaten the fruit, they felt guilty. They had done something God had asked them not to do. God knew they sinned. And they did, too. Their sin had a consequence—it broke their relationship with God."

All of them nodded their heads. They were really listening. I kept praying, and God kept putting thoughts into my mind and words into my mouth …

"Adam and Eve could no longer enjoy the pain-free life they had in the Garden of Eden. God put them out of the Garden that very day. Life became hard for them and for all people. Because they disobeyed God, sin, pain, suffering, and hardships came into the entire world. But, God did not leave them or forsake them. He still loved them. So He made a promise to send His very own Son, Jesus, to this earth to rescue them—and us—from our sin, death, and separation from God."

"We know from God's Word, the Bible, and from history books and records that God did keep His promise. He sent Jesus! Jesus was born in Bethlehem. He lived and walked on this earth, teaching about God, His Father. He went about serving and helping people, praying for them and doing miracles. Then, on what we know as Good Friday, Jesus hung on the cross, suffered, died, and was buried. It was a terrible, terrible day for His friends and family. But someone had to take the consequences of our sins in our place. Although Jesus, God's own Son, was perfectly innocent, He willingly took our place on the cross. Our dirty 'plates' of sin were put on Him. He became 'sin' for us.

"Because Jesus took our sin on Himself, He was separated from our Heavenly Father so we wouldn't have to be. As the Bible says, *'We all, like sheep, have gone astray, each of us has turned to his own way; and the LORD has laid on him the iniquity of us all.'* (Isaiah 53:6) At the end of His suffering on the cross, He said, *'It is finished.'* (John 19:30) Those words meant 'paid in full.' Jesus fully paid the price for our sin. Then, three days later, Jesus rose again—he came up and out of the grave! He conquered sin, death, and the evil one, too. Because of what He did, Jesus can wipe all the dirt off our plates, all the sin off our hearts. We can be made clean as we turn away from our sin and turn to Jesus as our Savior. We can have a relationship with Him now and eternal fellowship with our Father in Heaven forever!"

I could see a look of hope start to appear on the faces of these young women. They had gone through many experiences of pain and loss in their lives. At this moment, they were hearing the good news of God's love and care for them. The Savior wanted them to come to Him. I knew I couldn't stop now…

"Before Jesus left the earth and went back up into Heaven, He made a promise. He said that a Helper, the Holy Spirit, would come and give faith and power to His followers. The Holy Spirit would enable all who trust in Christ to do far greater things than Jesus Himself had done. Then Jesus gave His disciples a mission, a purpose, in life. He said: *Therefore go and make disciples of all nations, baptizing them in the name of the Father and of the Son and of the Holy Spirit, and teaching them to obey everything I have commanded you. And surely I am with you always, to the very end of the age.' (Matthew 28:19–20) After Jesus said these words, He returned to Heaven. The disciples spent the next ten days together, praying and waiting for the Holy Spirit to come.* After ten days, God's Holy Spirit was poured out upon them, and upon thousands of others, in an event called Pentecost."

As we sat quietly together in that dimly lit room, I could sense the presence of the Holy Spirit enlightening the hearts of the six young women who were listening closely to the words God was giving me to speak to them…

"Think about it. Jesus is offering you a gift. It is the gift of faith, forgiveness, abundant life today, and life with Him forever in Heaven. On the cross, Jesus paid for this gift with his perfect life. He paid the price you could never pay. *For it is by grace you have been saved, through faith—and this not from yourselves, it is the gift of God—not by works, so that no one can boast.'* (Ephesians 2:8–9) You can't receive this gift by trying really hard to be good, because none of us can ever be good enough. You can only receive this gift by faith—by trusting not in yourself or in what you have done, but by trusting in Jesus and what He did for you on the cross. The Holy Spirit is the One who creates this faith in your heart as you hear about Jesus."

I asked them to picture Jesus standing at the door of their hearts, knocking and offering them this free gift. I knocked on my journal. Tap, tap, tap. I said, "He's knocking on the door of each one of your hearts. He loves you and wants to come into your life." Then I went on to tell them what had happened to me as a child…

"When I was a young girl, about ten or eleven years old, I read the words of Jesus in the Bible: *'Here I am! I stand at the door and knock. If anyone hears my voice and opens the door, I will come in and eat with him and he with me.'* (Revelation 3:20) The Holy Spirit worked through these words and gave me faith to trust in Jesus alone. To put it another way, He gave me the power to do something I never could have done by myself—to open the door of my heart and ask Jesus to come and live in me as my Savior. At that moment I had such peace and joy. I wanted Him to change my life. I wanted to learn as much as I could from Him. So, I kept reading the Bible, praying, and going to church and Sunday school. Oh, yes, I still sometimes fought with my sisters and brother, and sinned in other ways. But I learned to tell Jesus about it and to ask Him for His forgiveness. He always 'cleaned my plate' with His forgiveness and helped me make better choices as I learned more and more from His Word."

Here I was, in the words of the old song, "I Love to Tell the Story," telling *"the old, old story of Jesus and His love."* In that little candlelit room, God was empowering me to share with these young African girls who were truly hungering after the spiritual truths of the Bible. By the leading of His Holy Spirit I had long ago trusted in Jesus, the One who came into my heart and life. Now I asked them if this was something they wanted to do.

And they did! By His grace and through the power of His Holy Spirit, God worked new and deeper faith in their hearts. They repented of their sins, confessed their faith in Jesus, and received His forgiveness. After we prayed, I shared with them the confirming promise of God's Word: *"Believe in the Lord Jesus, and you will be saved—you and your household."* (Acts 16:31) There was a lot of hugging, crying, giggling, and whispering. It was truly a "Hallelujah!" moment for me.

Finally we all crawled into our beds. I lay there in the darkness, tucked in and moved to tears. Thinking of the way the Lord had moved in the hearts of these young women, I was very humbled by what had happened. I knew that God had done it all, bringing some of them to faith in Christ and giving others of them a greater assurance of their faith in Him. After a while, I prayed, *"Quiet my thoughts, Lord."* Even with all the adrenaline pumping through me, that's just what He did. Soon I was fast asleep.

But not for long. When the 4:00 a.m. horn blew, I was up. I spent the first part of Sunday morning talking and praying with Rose, the colonel and some his soldiers, and then going with Moses, Kathy and Bob to the radio station. Upon our return to the house after the broadcast, I went back toward my room and heard lots of giggling. I knew something was going on with the young women. I knocked on the door. Upon opening the door, they grabbed me and hugged me. I felt such a special bond with them after what had happened the night before. The Lord had done such a wonderful thing, and we all still felt it. But right now they were busy getting dressed for church and were very giddy with enthusiasm. There was definitely an extraordinary amount of excitement in the air. I thought to myself, *Hmm ... something must be going on.* I was reminded of how it was back home with my daughter's girlfriends all getting ready at the same time in her bedroom. I was taking it all in just watching them and having fun, when one of the girls entered the room carrying a dress. It was a purple, silvery-colored dress. I asked, "Is something going on today?"

They just looked at each other, laughed, and wouldn't tell me. All they said was, "It's a secret!" I was surprised when they put the dress over Mercy's head and then fixed her hair. She looked beautiful! I kept trying to pry out of them what was going on, but they wouldn't say a word. I sat there thinking about the initial feeling I had when I first met Mercy just the evening before. I thought to myself, *Isn't it interesting that the outfit the Lord impressed me to give to Mercy is also purple, with silvery and gold threads woven throughout?* I knew that I wasn't supposed to tell her, or anyone else, the thoughts God was putting in my mind. Instead, I was to keep praying and waiting on the Lord for His timing.

I left the girls and finished gathering my things. Before long, it was time to leave for the morning service at the tent church. I walked the short distance with Pastor Moses, Pastor Steve, Kathy, Bob, Rose, and all the kids. When we arrived, people were already streaming in and sitting on chairs lined up on the dirt floor. I sat up front with Kathy and Bob. While we waited, I prayed for the Holy Spirit to quiet my heart and prepare me with what He wanted me to teach that morning.

The service began with the most wonderful music and singing. Pastor Steve then stood up and asked a young man, Levi, to come to the front, along with several other men in the church who would pray for him. He announced that Levi was engaged to be married and was making it public in church that morning. I thought, *This is really, really cool.* Levi pulled a magenta-colored flower from a floral arrangement on the altar, turned, and started walking to the back of the tent. All eyes followed him. To my utter surprise, he handed the flower to Mercy! Smiling a huge smile, she stood up. Her face was absolutely glowing, and she looked stunning in her floor-length, silvery purple dress. Levi took Mercy by the hand and brought her up to the front of the church. The pastors and elders laid hands on them and prayed. Now I knew—this was the big secret! My heart was touched to be a part of this great blessing and to see this special moment in the lives of Mercy and Levi.

Mercy wearing her beautiful engagement dress.

As the worship service continued, we all had a turn to speak. I found it interesting that the Lord had showed me earlier that morning that I was to talk about the importance of personal holiness and purity. I shared how, with the Lord's help, my husband and I kept our purity with one another before we were married. I also talked about our wedding night, when we sat on the bed in our honeymoon suite in St. Louis, Missouri, and asked God to bless our marriage and to keep us faithful to one another. By His grace we had done that over all our years together. As I spoke, God pointed out to me that this was a message for the many couples there who were frequently apart from one another. Sometimes they were separated from each other for weeks and months on end, as husbands often had to work far away in order to provide for their families.

At the end of the four-hour-long service, we walked back to the compound and found many visitors already swarming the house for food and for time with us. We ate lunch, once again sharing plates. As I looked at the young women, I couldn't help but think about the talk we had together the night before, and I wondered what they remembered from it. After the crowd thinned out, I went back to my room. I needed time to pray and prepare for what I was to speak about that evening in the tent church.

When I opened the door, there sat Mercy. We hugged. She seemed a little nervous and embarrassed. I told her how well they had all kept the secret, and that they had really surprised me. She laughed. I told her how very beautiful she had looked in her dress, and she informed me she had worked for an entire year to pay for the dress and shoes she had worn that morning. Mercy bubbled over telling me all about Levi and his desire to become a minister. She said she was a little nervous about that, wanting to be a good wife for him. She also told me that they had prayed to stay pure in their relationship, and that what I shared in church that morning had meant so much to her. I assured her that as long as she and Levi kept Jesus at the center of their relationship, God would help them. I could see why the Lord had chosen her to be the recipient of the purple skirt outfit: she truly wanted to be a woman of faith and prayer, depending on the Lord for and in all things. I told her how I had immediately sensed a connection with her the first time we met, and somehow I knew we would be friends.

Then a thought came into my mind. I asked, "Mercy, if you could have anything in the world, what would you want?" The words were scarcely out of my mouth when she answered me. "A Bible. That's what I want!" She told me she wanted to read it like she had seen me read my Bible. How awesome is that? Mercy didn't know it, but I had a few scarcely used Bibles left, from all of the ones people back home had given me. I pulled out one of these Bibles from my bag and gave it to her.

Mercy grabbed the Bible and held it close to her heart. She asked if I could teach her how to study it. My heart leapt—here was a woman thirsting after God's Word! So, right then and there, I showed her my Bible and explained to her how I would underline verses that seemed important to me. I also showed her little notes I had written on the margins of my Bible during a Bible study or a sermon. Picking up the journal that I was using for this trip, I pointed out some of the things I had written in it—special verses the Lord had given to me, names of people from different countries, prayer requests and things I was thankful for. It came to me to give this journal to Mercy, so I tore out the pages I had already written on and gave the rest of it to her. She was grinning from ear to ear. We hugged a long time. It was a cherished moment God gave me with an extraordinary young woman, one who wanted to learn more and more of God's Word. I said a prayer for Mercy, and then it was time for us to freshen up before going to church.

Praying in the Sunday night service at the tent church.

After coming back from the tent church later that evening, I was still on "cloud nine." I had seen the Lord pour out His presence and His Spirit throughout the entire evening. I was numb and "done in"—totally wiped out. After everything that had happened, I didn't even feel like eating—so I gave hugs to all the little ones and said my good nights. Rose hugged me again with her giant squeeze and gave me a lit candle for my room.

Planting the candle on the shelf in my bedroom, I got ready for bed, longing for some much-needed sleep. As I tucked my mosquito net into place, my mind was still racing, remembering the stories wrapped around all the dear people who had come forward for prayer that evening in church. There were so many people who waited and

122

waited in line for prayer. Among them was Grace, and my thoughts now turned to her. She was one of the six young women I had talked with the previous night. The colonel and Rose had rescued her from the streets of Kampala, and she was sharing one of the bunk beds in my room. When Grace had come forward in church that evening, I asked her how I could pray for her. Instantly, she broke open with a torrent of emotion. Through her tears, she told me that not only had her husband died of AIDS, but two of her children had also died of AIDS. And she had recently found out she, too, had AIDS, as well as her last surviving child. I listened carefully as she spoke in broken English. I didn't want to miss a word of what she was saying. With the Spirit's help, I asked for healing to come into her body and also the body of her infant son, who was already in a local hospital. I thought of Mercy and the other young women who slept in this room. I prayed: *"Help them, Lord. I'm so thankful for the time we had together last night. How You were preparing me and them for all that has since taken place! They told You that they were sorry for the sins of their past. They received Your forgiveness; best of all, they received You by faith. You, Jesus, came into their hearts! Now, Lord, Grace is praying for healing. Thank You that You alone are able to do immeasurably more than we could ask or even imagine."*

As I was praying, I heard the creaking of the door slowly opening. It was Mercy. She didn't want to disturb me, but she asked if we could talk. In my mind, I thought: *I can sleep when I get home....* I didn't want to miss out on yet another opportunity God was giving to me.

Mercy looked so serious. I motioned for her to sit down. She sat on the edge of the bed. With tears rolling down her cheeks, she said something very unexpectedly had happened to her in church that evening. While we were praying for people, she too was praying, and a thought came into her mind to do something. She had already talked to Levi about it. This piqued my interest, and I was eager to hear what the Lord had impressed upon her heart. She said she believed God was telling her to give away her beautiful engagement dress, the one she'd worn that morning in church. She said the thought and feeling just wouldn't go away. She felt she was to give her engagement dress to us, and we were to give it to someone who needed it when we visited the refugee camp in Gulu.

I was surprised and caught off guard. Mercy's generosity overwhelmed me. This was no small thing for her to do. Not only had she worked almost an entire year to pay for her purple dress, there were also many emotional attachments connected to it. Giving away her engagement dress, after having worn it only once, would be an unbelievable sacrifice for her. I asked her what Levi had said. He had told her if she believed it was what God wanted her to do, she should do it. I thought, *Praise God! That's very sound counsel. Levi is an honorable man, to be sure. No wonder these two are engaged.* I had learned that it's always good to talk over decisions you are contemplating with the people who are also involved in what you are doing. It's also good to ask godly people for counsel and prayer. That's just what Mercy was doing, right then with me. So I told her to take time and sleep on it and not to rush into a decision. That would just be reacting to a thought. I encouraged her to pray and wait on the Lord. If, after she did that, she still felt the same way and had peace about it, she should do what she believed God was telling her to do. I lifted the mosquito net, took her hands, and we hugged and prayed together.

The whole time we were doing this, I was thinking to myself, *Mercy doesn't even know about this amazing purple outfit I have for her!* I understood now why the Lord had not allowed me to give it to her yet, or to even to talk with her about all the skirts I had been giving away in Africa. God wanted her to learn the wonderful joy of giving away something very special—something that was of great value and held so much meaning—without knowing how He would provide from there. He wanted Mercy and Levi to experience the joy of listening, obeying, and giving sacrificially by faith. In my heart, I said to the Lord, *I'm so, so, so glad I didn't jump ahead of You. Thank You for teaching me to wait on You. Thank You for this confirmation about giving Mercy the purple skirt. I know You are near me and are guiding me. God, You are so good!*

Early the next morning, I had to do things quietly and quickly in order to be ready when Moses arrived with a taxi to take us to meet with the major general. When I was dressed and ready I slipped out of the room, so as not to wake the girls. I went out into the courtyard, climbed into a tiny, old, beaten-up taxi and off we went. Eight hours later, we returned with the major general's enormous blue truck, driven by his personal driver. As everyone gathered around, we excitedly explained to them the miraculous things God had done that day.

As we were talking, I spotted Mercy. I could tell by the look on her face that she needed to talk. The two of us hurried into the house, down the hall, and into our room. We pushed back the mosquito netting and plunked down on the bed, just like bosom-buddy friends. She grabbed the Bible I'd given her the night before. With excitement clearly evident on her face, she showed me a passage the Lord had led her to that morning. To my surprise, she turned to Matthew 25:40: "*The King will reply, 'I tell you the truth, whatever you did for one of the least of these bothers of mine, you did for me.'*" Mercy had underlined those words. I was so proud of her that she was already putting into practice what I'd shown her about spending time in God's Word. She knew she now had God's answer about her purple dress. She said, "I'm giving it away." The Holy Spirit had confirmed it to her through His words right there in the Bible. Her heart was absolutely ready to let go of her precious dress. She cried. I cried! I took her pencil and showed her how to write the day's date next to Matthew 25:40 in the margin of her Bible, along with a note that this was the day God gave her confirmation about giving away her purple engagement dress. It would remind her of the day she gave away something of value and received great joy in return as she responded obediently to the Lord's prompting with no-holds-barred giving. In the journal I gave her, Mercy had copied the words of Matthew 25:40 and wrote what she was going to do. As she was showing me this, I sensed the Lord saying, *Now! Now is the time!*

I certainly knew what that meant! I said, "Just a minute, Mercy." Hopping off the bed, I unlocked my suitcase and pulled out the bag containing the expensive-looking, beautiful vest and skirt—woven with purple, gold, and silver strands all intertwined. I told Mercy all about God leading me to give away skirts from women in America to women in Africa. I opened the bag and showed her the note pinned inside the skirt. This skirt was given by Ann, a generous and wealthy woman. She was a woman of strong faith, and an intercessory prayer warrior. I told Mercy how I would pray about what skirt to wear each day and how God would impress me with which skirt to wear. The Lord had led me to wear this particular purple outfit on a Sunday morning in Pastor Angelo's church in Mombassa, even though I had to pin it on both sides because it was way too big for me. I described to Mercy the way God had worked that morning in Mombassa, how I had first held back from giving what the Lord asked me to give, and how I confessed that to the church and then put all my schillings into the purple hat. I told her of the resulting response from the people as they came forward, confessed to the pastor, and filled the purple hat several times over with money they had been holding back from giving to the Lord—enough money to supply the needs of the church for at least an entire year!

I went on and shared with Mercy how I had thought about giving this purple skirt outfit to women in other countries on our trip, but each and every time the Lord had said, "*Wait. It isn't time yet.*" So, I kept waiting and kept praying every day. Then came the day when we arrived at the colonel and Rose's house. I told Mercy that the very moment I saw her, I immediately sensed God's Spirit saying to me: "*It's her! She's the one!*" But I also knew that I needed to pray and wait for confirmation from the Lord about the right time to give the skirt outfit to her.

As I was speaking, Mercy began to cry. I looked into her tear-filled eyes and said words similar to this: "When things unfolded the next day in church, I had absolutely no idea of your engagement with Levi or anything about your purple dress. I knew nothing, nothing at all about it. But the Lord knew. I wanted to tell you about my purple outfit while you were praying about giving away your purple dress, but the Lord wouldn't let me. He kept saying, '*Wait. Wait.*' He just wouldn't release me to give it to you. Now, I know why. This outfit was to go to someone who is a strong woman of faith, prayer, and generosity. You are that woman! You were listening to His prompting when He put that crazy and unexpected thought into your mind—to give away your very special dress, after wearing it only one time. It seemed so unbelievable! But you kept on praying. You knew what to do, and you did it. You gave your dress away with a cheerful heart out of joy and obedience to God's voice. So, now, dear sweet Mercy, the Lord wants you to have this skirt outfit. He had me save it just for you. It is a symbol of love and obedience, a blessing coming back to you, and a confirmation that the Lord knows of your tremendous sacrifice of love."

We both sat there looking at each other, quietly absorbing the enormity of what had happened. God's Spirit was electrifyingly present, enveloping us in that breathtaking moment. He had done it all, starting all the way back in America with Ann, who had first pulled that purple skirt outfit from her closet to send to someone in Africa. I knew she had been praying for me for weeks, asking the Holy Spirit to lead me to give it to the exact woman He had chosen. And, just as He had spoken to Ann, He had also spoken to Mercy as well as to me!

Overcome with joy and thanksgiving, Mercy and I prayed together. After we prayed, I gave her a periwinkle-colored shirt to wear with the skirt and vest. She left the room to try it on. In no time at all she was back, wearing the entire purple outfit. No safety pins were needed—it was a perfect fit. Mercy looked beautiful! We hugged, knowing this was a moment neither one of us would ever forget.

If you want to pray, listen, and respond to God...
Commit yourself to be sacrificially generous with God
and with others.

CHAPTER SIX - REFLECTION PAGES

"Commit yourself to be sacrificially generous with God and with others."

PRAY AND LISTEN TO GOD AS YOU READ THESE WORDS FROM THE BIBLE

1 John 4:9–12

This is how God showed his love among us: He sent his one and only Son into the world that we might live through him. This is love: not that we loved God, but that he loved us and sent his Son as an atoning sacrifice for our sins. Dear friends, since God so loved us, we also ought to love one another. No one has ever seen God; but if we love one another, God lives in us and his love is made complete in us.

1 John 3:16–18

This is how we know what love is: Jesus Christ laid down his life for us. And we ought to lay down our lives for our brothers. If anyone has material possessions and sees his brother in need but has not pity on him, how can the love of God be in him? Dear children, let us not love with words or tongue but with actions and in truth.

2 Corinthians 8:1–3a

And now, brothers, we want you to know about the grace that God has given the Macedonian churches. Out of the most severe trial, their overflowing joy and their extreme poverty welled up in rich generosity. For I can testify that they gave as much as they were able, and even beyond their ability.

Proverbs 11:25

A generous man will prosper; he who refreshes others will himself be refreshed

Luke 6:38

Give, and it will be given to you. A good measure, pressed down, shaken together and running over, will be poured into your lap. For with the measure you use, it will be measured to you.

Acts 20:35
In everything I did, I showed you that by this kind of hard work
we must help the weak, remembering the words the Lord Jesus
himself said: "It is more blessed to give than to receive."

Psalm 123:1–2
I lift up my eyes to you, to you whose throne is in heaven.
As the eyes of slaves look to the hand of their master, as the
eyes of a maid look to the hand of her mistress, so our eyes
look to the Lord our God, till he shows us mercy.

QUESTIONS FOR REFLECTION AND DISCUSSION

1. Are you, by God's grace, personally trusting in Jesus—and His sacrifice for you on the cross—for the forgiveness of your sins and a new life with the Lord forever? If so, describe how God worked this faith in your heart. *(If you currently are not trusting in Christ as your Savior, and this is something you desire to do by God's grace, you can pray right now the Prayer of Response that follows these questions.)*

2. How does praying, listening, and responding to God help you grow in living a life of extraordinary generosity?

3. Why do you think that, as Jesus said, "It is more blessed to give than to receive" (Acts 20:25)?

4. Describe a time when you prayerfully listened and responded to the Holy Spirit's prompting, and did something sacrificially generous. How were you and others blessed by this leading from the Lord?

5. Read the account of the poor widow in Mark 12:41–44. How was Mercy in this skirt story like this widow, and what was the result of her faith and obedience?

6. Can you find yourself anywhere in this skirt story? If so, please explain.

7. Spend time in prayer asking the Lord to make you more attentive to His promptings to be generous, just as a servant girl keeps her eyes on her mistress, watching for the slightest signal.

PRAYER OF RESPONSE

Heavenly Father, thank You so much for the sacrifice of your Son, Jesus, for me and for all people. By the power of your Holy Spirit, I ask You to forgive all of my sins, and I put my trust in Jesus alone as my Savior. As I have been loved by You, cause me to have a greater love for You and for others. Grow in me the faith-filled, risk-taking, and extravagant generosity I see in Your Son's life and in the lives of Mercy and the poor widow. Lead me to not only speak to You more and more, but also to listen and hear Your voice speaking to me. Help me to wait for a signal from You to act, and to act not in my time but Yours. Enable me to be sensitive and obedient to Your Spirit nudging me. May people see Jesus— and His boundless mercy and love—brightly displayed in my life for Your Glory and for the blessing of many. I pray this in the name of Your Son, Jesus, who gave His all for me. Amen!

CHAPTER SEVEN

SKIRT STORY NUMBER SIX—
MARILYN

If you want to pray, listen, and respond to God…
Have a passionate desire to see people come to know the
eternal love of Jesus Christ.

S tanding in the front courtyard of the colonel and Rose's house, we watched as the soldiers loaded up the last of our things onto the bed of the major general's truck. The bed of the truck was filled with our bags and containers, along with many donations of food, toys, and clothes from the people of the tent church there in Kampala. Also in the back of the truck was the bag containing Mercy's beautiful purple engagement dress. In my mind I prayed, *Lord, You already know who will get that dress given out of joy and obedience by Mercy and Levi. Bless them, Lord, and bless the woman who will ultimately receive it. Thank you for working out your will through a simple thing like a purple skirt and dress, and for showing me the blessing of praying, waiting, and listening for Your promptings.*

While the soldiers were tying an orange tarp over everything in the back of the truck, several of the children ran over to me and each gave me one of the few special treasures or trinkets they possessed. They also pressed into my hands notes that they'd written on tiny pieces of paper, along with pictures they had drawn. While kneeling down to receive these loving mementos, I fought back tears, hugging and thanking each one of them for their simple but generous expressions of love to me. They truly were gifts from the heart!

Mercy, with the other young women, walked over to me. The atmosphere was thick with emotion. We all stood there feeling heavyhearted and struggling to find words to express our feelings. We were all thinking back over the events of the past three days; it was amazing what the Lord had done. So many answered prayers! So many new professions of faith in Christ! So many new friends and memories! Realizing we might never see each other again this side of heaven, we stood encircled, with our arms on each others' shoulders and our heads tucked down. We did a group hug and squeeze, feeling each other's emotions while saying, "I'll never forget you!" and "I love you!"

I looked over at Rose and marveled at how God had answered her persistent prayers for the salvation of her husband. She had never given up her passionate desire to see the colonel come to know Jesus as his Savior. And now, a new life was beginning for both of them—a dream come true. There would be challenges and they would need God's help, but I knew Rose's faith and her prayer life would continue to prevail. For me, the colonel's transformation was a moment I will never forget. I was deeply humbled and affected by what had happened. The Lord had done it all, enabling me by His Spirit, not by my own strength. I had witnessed Him do more than I could ever have imagined.

A few more pictures were taken, and then it was time for us to go. Concerned for our safety, the major general had sent over another armed soldier to accompany us on our trip. So we asked everyone—including the major general's driver, Henry, and the two soldiers—to join hands and make a prayer circle around the truck. Several of us prayed, thanking the Lord for the many ways He had worked during our time in Kampala. We asked for His continued blessings on Rose, the colonel, and their household. Lastly, we prayed for God's protection over us, for His angels to surround us, and for His Spirit to lead us wherever He wanted us to go during our journey to the refugee camps.

Henry motioned to the guards to open the heavy red metal gate. The screeching sound of the gate sliding open signaled that it truly was time to go. I stood there frozen, not really wanting to leave. But, after taking one last look at the tear-stained faces of Rose, Mercy, and all the women and children, I climbed into the backseat of the major general's truck, followed by Kathy and Bob. Pastor Moses got in the front seat next to Henry. The two armed guards stationed themselves on the back bed of the truck.

With a beep-beep of the horn, Henry pulled out of the courtyard onto the rough dirt road. We were on our way to Gulu, Uganda—210 miles north of Kampala. Feeling an emotional letdown, I sank into the corner of the backseat. I didn't want to leave what had become the familiar safety of the colonel's home. It was hard to say goodbye to all my new friends who were so teachable and hungry to learn from God's Word. But I knew that we had something very significant ahead of us. Over the next three days we would have a lot of miles to cover and ministry to do before returning to Nairobi, Kenya, for our flight home. I prayed, *"God, You promised that I can do all things because You strengthen me. Help me to set my heart and mind upon You, and sustain me with Your strength!"*

The major general's truck load as we prepared to leave for Gulu.

Henry was very familiar with the road to Gulu. Riding in the major general's truck, we were waved through all the checkpoints without having to make any stops whatsoever. These little "nobodies" by the world's standards were being treated like "somebodies." I couldn't help but compare this ride with the arduous and rugged bus ride we'd taken from Rwanda to Kampala just three days before. God knew that our exhausted bodies needed this!

Bob, Kathy, and I fell asleep for a couple of hours. We woke when Henry stopped the truck on a bridge overlooking the fast-moving waters of the Victoria Nile, a massive river in Uganda that forms the upper section of the Nile River. What a sight! The rough waters made me think of the movie, *The African Queen,* with Humphrey Bogart and Katherine Hepburn, parts of which had been filmed in Uganda. Just as in the movie, the river was surrounded by jungle, reminding us that much of Africa is still an untamed country. It was a breathtaking view. After stretching our legs and taking a few photos, we climbed back into the truck, knowing we still had miles to travel before we arrived at our destination.

As we drove along, Pastor Moses told us about the horrific civil war that had been going on for almost twenty years in northern Uganda and southern Sudan. A group of rebels calling themselves the Lord's Resistance Army (LRA) had been responsible for the abduction of nearly 20,000 children. Horrifyingly these children were torn from their homes, after the rebels maimed or executed their parents. The rebels brainwashed the boys and trained them to use weapons; these boys eventually made up 80 percent of the LRA military. Some of the young girls who were abducted with them were forced to become sex slaves. The LRA had been responsible for the murder of nearly 100,000 people in northern Uganda and southern Sudan. Adding to this tragedy was the massive psychological damage inflicted on hundreds of thousands of other people as well.

In response to this, the government of Uganda forced nearly two million northern Ugandans to leave their homes, putting them into camps called Internal Displacement Camps (IDPs). This was supposedly for their protection. Sadly, some government troops took advantage of the situation, not only pillaging and stealing the homes left behind but also raping young girls and women in the camps. Pastor Moses told us that 90 percent of the population of northern Uganda had been displaced to around 250 refugee camps. To make matters even worse, refugees from South Sudan were also flooding into these Ugandan camps. At the time of our visit, the camps had some of the highest mortality rates in the world; the Ugandan Ministry of Health estimated that 1,000 people were dying weekly in these camps, mostly from malaria, cholera, and AIDS. Not only that, the Lord's Resistance Army would sometimes attack these camps, taking even more lives.

Pabbo, one of the two camps we were going to, was the largest IDP. It was built to hold 10,000 people, but housed almost 70,000 people. Around 80 percent of these were women and children. There were very few men or boys. Grandparents were forced to raise their grandchildren, as many of the parents had been killed. In describing all of this, it was evident to me that Pastor Moses was preparing us for the dire conditions we would be encountering during our time in the refugee camps.

Knowing I had trouble with motion sickness in the backseat, Pastor Moses offered to exchange places with me so that I could sit in the front seat of the truck. I knew this wasn't a coincidence—I had been praying for an opportunity to get to know our driver, Henry, and this was it. Even though I was feeling exhausted from a lack of sleep and and nauseous from the swaying movements of the truck, I shot up a prayer, *Thank You, Lord, for bringing this good out of my motion sickness!* I sat down in the front seat and asked Henry to tell me about himself. Henry spoke very good English, in addition to his native language, Swahili. Pulling pictures out of his shirt pocket, his eyes sparkled and danced as he told me all about his beautiful wife and infant son. Regrettably, Henry didn't get to see them every day, which made him very sad. But he told me that he felt extremely "lucky" to have such an honorable job being the major general's driver. He shared with me stories of how, whenever he was with the major general, he was treated very well and always had plenty of food to eat. I boldly told him that there was no such thing as "luck" or "coincidences," but that it was actually the Lord who had led the major general to choose him to be his driver. I explained that God was the One who was at work in his life, not only giving him the skills to drive but also directing the major general—who was a man of God—to choose Henry to be his very own personal driver. I was speaking frankly with Henry, and he was attentive to every word I shared.

It was clear to me that God was preparing both Henry and me for a deeper conversation about Jesus—a conversation I hoped to have with him during our trip to the refugee camps. My time in Africa would soon be drawing to a close, and I kept praying for more opportunities to speak God's Word to others. I wanted to proclaim the good news of what Jesus had done for all people, and to pray with those whose hearts the Holy Spirit had prepared to trust in Jesus as their Savior. I sensed the Lord was drawing me to this young man; he was the same age that my son, Adam, would have been. As Henry and I talked, I prayed, *Give me Your words, Jesus, and give me the right time to share them with Henry.*

Getting closer to the Pabbo refugee camp, we arrived in the city of Gulu. This city, with its population of over 100,000 people, is the largest city in northern Uganda. Gazing out the window, I could see that a large proportion of the Gulu population still lived in grass-thatched huts. Onlookers stopped and stared at our loaded-down, well-guarded truck as we drove down the dirt roads, stirring up clouds of red dust. Henry dodged the walkers and bike riders and pulled up to a gated motel, where we got out of the truck and made arrangements to stay for the next two nights.

I found it interesting how quickly things can move when you have military guards assisting. They helped us unload the last of our bags from the truck bed, and carried them into our small rooms. While standing over one of the two twin-sized beds in the room I was sharing with Kathy, I made a conscious decision to not give any thought to whoever might have slept in that bed before me. After seeing all the tin and cardboard houses with thatched roofs while we drove through town, I was just thankful to have a room with a door and a lock on it. Kathy and I quickly gathered up our bags, purchased some bottled water from the kitchen to keep us from getting dehydrated, and headed back out to the major general's truck so we could drive over to the military base. The major general had instructed us to check in at this base. Upon our arrival there, we would need to fill out paperwork to get the proper clearances necessary to enter two of the refugee camps the next morning. The general also wanted to make sure we would have additional military guards accompanying us, as there were rebels hiding in the bush and attacking people all along the route into the camps.

I once again climbed into the front seat, next to Henry. As he drove us to the base, he asked me a lot of questions about what I had said earlier. He also wanted to know why the major general had given us the usage of the truck and his services. He mentioned that the general had never done anything like this before. I wanted to have more time to talk with Henry, but we were pulling up to the entrance gate of the base compound. The guards at the gate saw our official vehicle and waved us through without any questions. I smiled, thinking about the kind of treatment we were being given. I knew it wasn't a "lucky" coincidence; instead, it was God's grace-filled answer to the many prayers people were praying for us.

When we reached the administrative offices, Pastor Moses, Bob, and Kathy went inside to arrange for an appointment with the base commander. Because we'd have to wait for a while, Henry and I stood next to the truck and continued our one-on-one conversation. By now, Henry was anxious to talk about what he had experienced with us in recent days. He had been included in our times of singing and prayers at the colonel's house. He had heard me talk about the Lord at the tent church, as I spoke of the importance of praying with one's spouse and shared what my husband had done by writing those notes for me. He had heard how we'd sung "What a Friend We Have in Jesus," and how many people had come forward for prayer. Henry told me he had never been a part of anything like that before. He also told me that his wife was a Christian, but he wasn't. Having been exposed to Christianity, he wanted to know more about it.

So I seized the moment. I gave Henry a condensed version of how I ended up in Africa with Kathy and Bob, and without my friend, Barbara. I told him that the Lord had given me a verse from the Bible, and I shared with him the words of Joshua 1:9. I pointed out that God had asked me to be strong and courageous, and to look to Him for His help. God had been faithful to His promise and had done so many amazing things in the days I'd been in Africa. I reminded Henry that these were things that only a God like our Lord Jesus could orchestrate. And he, Henry, was obviously a part of what the Lord was doing for us. Henry was very focused on what I was saying. I was right on the verge of telling him the most important thing that Jesus had done for him, when a soldier opened the door and called us inside. I quickly prayed, *Oh, no, Lord, give me another chance to talk with Henry!* I didn't know it at the time, but before our trip to Gulu was over, the Lord would give me that very opportunity.

The young soldier led us down a hallway and into the stark offices of the base commander. I felt a little unworthy and unsure of myself as we stepped into a room where the base commander, as well as several other military officers, was sitting around a rectangular table. Clearly this was not an every day occurrence when simple folks like us showed up, unannounced, with the personal driver and guards of a major general. When we entered the room, the base commander and his officers respectfully stood up, bowed their heads, and greeted us. I knew that God was opening doors! After introductions were made, everyone sat back down around the table. We began telling them how we had ended up there, and exactly what we were planning to do in the camps. We explained that it was the major general who told us to come to the base in order to secure clearance and get additional military protection for our drive down the treacherous road into the Pabbo refugee camp.

Then, suddenly, out of nowhere, came an excruciatingly loud sound. It reminded me of the blaring tornado sirens I used to hear back home in Texas. I stayed composed, but I could feel my heart racing and pounding rapidly. Filled with fear, almost simultaneously I prayed, *"Help us, Lord!"* For a moment, no one moved. Then the officer who had introduced himself as the "on call" doctor jumped up and hurried out of the room. Immediately after that came another much louder, booming siren. It was so loud that it hurt my ears. Putting my hands over my ears, I glanced out the window. I saw a number of soldiers carrying weapons and equipment running toward several aircraft, one of which was a medevac helicopter, identified by a large red cross painted on its side.

Clearly, something big was going on. I wanted to ask what was happening, but I kept quiet. I prayed, knowing that was the best thing to do. The "on call" doctor, with his gear in hand, stuck his head back into the room and looked directly at us. Almost frantically, he said in broken English, "Are you sure you want to go into the camps?" Then off he went, without saying another word. Seeing the desperate look on his face, my heart sank. I began to wonder if we would even get to go into the camps. I kept on praying, *"Lord, You know our heart's desire. We have come a long way to get here. Please allow us to get in."* Pastor Moses, Bob, Kathy and I sat there almost frozen, speechless and wide-eyed, looking at each other, unsure of what was happening next. That's when a soldier came into the room. He informed the base commander and the officers that there had been an attack and help was needed. Obviously the meeting was over. And it looked like our plans to visit the refugee camps were over, too. But miraculously, when we stepped out of the room and into the hallway, we were handed all the clearances we needed to go to the camps the next morning. In addition to that, following the major general's orders, four more armed soldiers would provide additional security for us when we would go into the camps.

Days later, we found out what had happened while we were in the base commander's office—a van filled with volunteer aid workers driving into the refugee camps had been attacked by rebels. Every one of the workers had been killed. They didn't have any military protection, and they were traveling on the exact same road we would be taking into the camps. Now we understood why the major general had been so adamant about providing us with not just one, or two, or even three armed soldiers, but with six! I was filled with awe and wonder at the mighty hand of God continually at work, intervening on our behalf and providing us with protection for our safety.

Even today, the Lord's words keep coming back to my mind, ringing in my ears as I am reminded of God's promise to me: *You will have all that you need, when you need it!* and, *I am able to do abundantly more than what you ask or even imagine!* We weren't able, but God was able. We didn't know, but He knew. God used not only the major general but also Rose's husband, the colonel, to provide all that we needed when we needed it; they were, no doubt, a Godsend. I believe that our very lives were saved because God had provided them to us. We didn't know that rebels were hiding in the tall grass all along the roadway to the refugee camps, ready to attack unguarded people. On our own we never would have thought to get military protection, much less known how to go about securing it. But God knew! And He made it happen for us. He is a God of the details! He sees and knows what we can't see. We may have a plan, but God directs our path and He uses people along the way to accomplish it. Thank you, Jesus, for your attention to every single detail of our lives!

After gathering all the necessary paperwork for our visit to the camps the next day, we thanked the commander and once again piled into the major general's truck, heading back to the motel. Having been invited to speak in a worship service at a church in Gulu, we would have only a short time to get ready for that. By now I was getting used to speaking with only a moment's notice, calling upon the Lord for direction. Once inside my room at the motel, I sat on my bed's thin, lumpy mattress.

There was only one source of light in the room—a single bulb hanging lopsided from the ceiling and casting shadows on the walls. The air was stale and warm. I knew I had to be careful, for I could have very easily curled up and fallen asleep. But, as tired as I was, I didn't want to pass up another opportunity for the Lord to fulfill my dream of teaching in Africa. I asked Him, *What shall I teach, and will I be giving away my sister Jan's skirt tonight?* At first there was silence. Nothing came. Then I had a thought: *Hmmm ... the Lord had told me to "remember."* So, I began thanking the Lord that He had helped me in the past and would once again show me what to say and do when I needed it. I read a passage in the Bible and reread my husband's note to me for the day. I knew that he and other faithful friends were still praying for me. As I combed my matted hair I continued praying, trying not to think about how bad my hair looked or how much it needed a good washing. That wasn't the need of the hour! Thinking of the people who would be in church that night, I said, *"I need Your help, Lord. Take my mind off how I look. Give me Your words to penetrate their hearts. Thank You for always being here for me. There's no one else just like You."*

Bob knocked on the door. It was time to depart for the church. Before leaving the room, I felt a nudge—an inner voice I knew to be the Holy Spirit—telling me to pull an item from my bag that I had packed before leaving my home in California. So I obediently put the item in my small tote bag, along with my Bible and my plastic water bottle. Locking the door behind me, I walked quickly to the major general's truck. As we pulled away from the motel, I inquired of Henry if he would be staying for church. He kept his eyes on the road and simply nodded his head up and down.

The church wasn't far from where we were staying. Looking out the window of the truck, I noticed a lot of young families walking alongside the road carrying infants and trying to corral their running happy, squealing children. Pastor Moses said they were coming to church to hear us speak. Upon arriving at the small cement church building, I followed Pastor Moses, Kathy and Bob into an opening on the side wall. I could already hear the methodical beating of the drums and the joyful sound of people's voices coming from within the church. As we stepped inside, through the dim light I could see rows and rows of narrow wooden benches already filled with people. Many others were sitting on colorful blankets spread around the dirt floors. It was really "wall to wall" people! I kept praying, *"Use me, Lord. Help me to show You to them."*

I followed Pastor Moses up to the front where a lectern was stationed. He introduced me to the pastor of the church and his wife—Pastor Jacob and Margaret. I immediately sensed God's presence in their instantaneous smiles, hugs, and enthusiastic words of welcome. It was evident to me that the Lord was at work in this church, and also working through this pastor and his wife. Pastor Jacob and Margaret showed us to our seats. Then the worship began. Everyone jumped to their feet as rhythmic music, singing, clapping and dancing filled the crowded cement building. It was totally exhilarating for me to join them in singing some of the now-familiar songs of African worship. You simply couldn't sit still! As I had grown accustomed to this African culture, the world began to seem like a much smaller place to me. I thought about how wonderful Heaven will be when we hear the voices of all kinds of people singing praises to the Lord in their own native tongue.

After a long time of worship and singing, Pastor Jacob spoke, followed by Kathy and Bob. By now we were nearly two hours into the service, and the windowless room had become hot and stifling. I concluded that there was probably no time left for me to speak. But Pastor Jacob called me to step forward. He announced in Swahili that he would be my interpreter. I grabbed my bag and headed over to the lectern. I laid my Bible down while he told the church how far I'd come from my home in the United States, and that this was the longest time I'd ever been away from my home and family. Then Pastor Jacob asked what word I had to share.

I opened my mouth and began to speak the words the Holy Spirit was giving me: "Even though I come from the United States, I have problems. And you have problems, too. Certainly, my problems are different from your problems. In fact, no matter where we live on God's earth, we will have difficulties. Why is that? We have problems because sin came into the world in the Garden of Eden, through the first man and woman, Adam and Eve." I could see they were listening, so I said, "Just like you need help to deal with your problems and hardships every day, I need help, too. Do you know what I do to get help? I pray. And I read the Bible. Psalm 121:1–2 says, '*I will lift up my eyes to the hills—where does my help come from? My help comes from the LORD, the Maker of heaven and earth.*'" Already, people were saying "Amen! Hallelujah!" I held up my well-worn Bible. "You know why the pages of this Bible are falling apart? It's because I read this Bible. I ask God to lead me and teach me through it, to fill me up and show me what to do. I ask Him to help me to love others as He loves me."

Almost immediately an idea popped into my mind. I grabbed my bag and took out my water bottle, along with the item I had brought from the motel. I turned to a verse in the Bible and read, "*Blessed are those who hunger and thirst for righteousness, for they shall be satisfied.*" (Matthew 5:6 ESV) My mouth was parched and dry from the hot night and from the building that was packed with people. I needed a drink of water, and I knew everyone there was just as thirsty as I was. So I said, "If you are thirsty, raise your hand." Hands flew up in the air. Even the little kids raised their hands. "I know your mouths must be as dry as mine." They all nodded. I paused between thoughts, as Pastor Jacob interpreted. Then I explained: "The feeling you get when you are desperately thirsty—and want a cool drink of water—is the very same way God wants you to feel about picking up and reading the Bible. Jesus wants us to thirst after His Word! Just like drinking water satisfies your physical thirst and keeps your body alive, reading and studying God's Word satisfies, or quenches, your spiritual thirst and gives life to your soul. You need God's Word every day. It gives you direction. It tells you what to do and what not to do. It convicts you of your sin and leads you to repent. It gives you help, comfort, hope and encouragement each day. It satisfies your soul like nothing else can. Best of all, the Bible tells you about Jesus—why and how He came to earth from Heaven, and what He did for all people." I quoted Jesus in Revelation 22:17, "*Whoever is thirsty, let him come; and whoever wishes, let him take the free gift of the water of life.*"

Then I asked, "What did Jesus do for us?" A young man raised his hand, and I called on him. He eloquently said that Jesus suffered and died for us, carrying our sins on the cross, and then rose again from the dead. I said "Amen!" and everyone responded "Amen!" Then I explained,

"When you come to the Lord Jesus and trust in His love and forgiveness for you, you receive His gift of eternal salvation. The Bible says that you become a child of God. That's the Good News! Romans 10:13 promises: *'Everyone who calls on the name of the Lord will be saved.'*" Shouts of "Hallelujah!" echoed through the church.

With that, I held up the item I had brought with me—a dried-up, yellow sponge. I had a little child stand up and I rubbed the dry, scratchy sponge on his arm. He frowned and pulled his arm away. "I'm sorry," I said. "I know that didn't feel good." He nodded. "But, unless you fill a sponge with water, it's no good at all. You can't use it." I asked everyone to pretend they were "sponges." I also asked them to raise their hands if they wanted to tell others about Jesus. Up went their hands again! So I opened my bottle of water and said, "Now, pretend this water is the Word of God. In order for you to be able to tell others about Jesus— to tell them what He did on the cross, and how He can help us with our problems every day—you need to fill up on the living water of His Word." I poured the water out of the bottle and onto the sponge. Then I rubbed the sponge, now wet, on the little boy's arm. This time he smiled, and everyone laughed. That felt better!

After this, the Lord led me to pour even more water onto the sponge. I said, "When you tell someone 'Jesus loves you,' it's as though you are splashing out God's Word onto them. You are being used by God to share His love." I walked around swinging the sponge while squeezing it in my hand, splashing the people in the audience with droplets of water. As I did this, I spoke aloud truths of the Bible like: "*Jesus loves you! Jesus died to save you! Jesus hears you when you pray! Jesus never leaves you! Jesus cares for you! Jesus is with you always!*" All the kids were clapping, wanting me to splash them. Soon there was no water left in the sponge. I told them that I had to fill it back up with more water in order for it to be useable again. "So it is with us as 'people-sponges,'" I said. "We need to continually soak up God's Word from the Bible in order to be able to tell others about Jesus and bring life and refreshment to them." Just to see if they were listening, I asked them what happens if you try to use a dried-up sponge. Someone answered, "It scratches you!" "That's right!" I added, "So, don't be like a dried-up sponge scratching people with your own words. Instead, fill yourself up with the Word of God every day. And ask Jesus to use you to tell others about Him. Not only will He help you speak to others, He will also help you with your own problems, just as He helps me with mine. All this is because He loves you!"

Having said what I believed the Holy Spirit wanted me to say, I closed with a prayer. I asked everyone to repeat each phrase as Pastor Jacob interpreted. *"Dear Lord, Thank You for giving me Your Word. It is like water that gives me life. Help me to be thirsty each and every day to read the Bible. Enable me to be like a sponge, and use me to pass on to others what I receive from You. I know You love me. Thank You for saving me. In Jesus' name, Amen."* I went and sat down. After singing one more song, Pastor Jacob gave the church a word of blessing and thanked everyone for coming. It was dark as I stood at the door of the church and hugged people, saying goodbye. I knew the Lord had given me that simple message of the water and the sponge, and I was grateful and humbled by the look of understanding in the eyes of the many Ugandans gathered there. By God's grace, they truly "got it."

Because it was a pitch-black night and difficult to see where to walk, Henry got the general's truck and pulled it up right by door of the church. It was hard to leave, but we knew we would see Pastor Jacob and Margaret again the next evening for a farewell gathering. So off we went, back to the motel where we would be eating dinner. By now we were really hungry. We hurried to the kitchen area where our food was being prepared. We would be served family style, with large platters of chicken and red gravy, along with white rice, black beans, and boiled green bananas.

Before we all sat down, a tall Ugandan man, someone I hadn't yet met, was asked to say a dinner prayer. His name was Pastor Armstrong. Something stirred inside of me when he prayed. I could see that he was a humble, quiet man. For some reason I knew I needed to get to know him, and I was grateful when I ended up sitting next to him at our dinner table. I introduced myself and asked him to tell me about himself and his family. Pastor Armstrong shared with me that his wife's name was Marilyn, and that they had nine children. He was the pastor of the church located in the Pabbo refugee camp and would be leading us in worship there the next morning. He was obviously an honorable man of God who wanted to serve the Lord and tell people about Jesus.

I asked Pastor Armstrong to tell me about the challenges and blessings of pastoring a church in the refugee camp. As he talked, he spoke many words of love, admiration, and kindness about his wife, Marilyn, and the desire they both had to show Jesus' love to the displaced refugees and to the sick and hurting people who came into the camp. He described his wife's passionate commitment to be a woman of prayer. While he was speaking about Marilyn and their ministry together, a thought came into my mind. It was as if the Lord's voice was whispering into my heart, *She's the one!*

Ever since I had arrived in Africa, I had been repeatedly asking the Lord, "Who should get my sister Jan's skirt?" He had led me to wear her skirt on many of my toughest days. Wearing Jan's skirt was almost like a mantle of prayer, assuring me that she was always in vigilant intercession, covering me with her prayers. Even though Jan is small in stature, she is a gargantuan prayer warrior! She has been a total blessing to me in my life and to hundreds and hundreds of others. I had confidence the Lord would tell me sooner or later when it was time for me to let go of her skirt. I knew that Jan's skirt would be going to a godly woman, one whom the Holy Spirit wanted to encourage to stay steadfast in her praying. Having finally heard from God that Marilyn was this woman, I was excited and began to look forward to the moment I would be able to meet her and give her my sister's skirt.

Not long after dinner we left the kitchen area together, making our way through the darkness back to our rooms. We would be leaving very early the next morning for the refugee camps. Kathy and I cleaned up quickly, both too exhausted to talk. I had already pulled out of my bag the outfit belonging to Barbara that I had promised to wear in her place when we visited the camps. It was a bright magenta and purple-colored skirt and jacket. I also brought out the purple hat I'd worn back in Mombassa, Kenya. As we laid on our beds in the darkness, Kathy and I prayed together. We were acutely aware of the fact that the next day we would be seeing people who had lost everything and were living in some very horrific and depressing conditions. We desperately wanted to show them—and tell them—that they mattered to God and to us. Knowing I was someone who is prone to tears, I had asked people to pray specifically for me that day that I would not cry in the camps. Instead, the desire of my heart was for me to be able to share with people the love, joy, and hope of Jesus. I wanted to treat them as Jesus would—touching them, helping them, and praying for them.

Early the next morning, the sun was up when Kathy and I headed off to the kitchen for some fruit and toast. Already, four additional military guards were there, joining the two we already had. We got our food and sat down at a small table. When everyone had finished breakfast, all of us gathered for prayer around the major general's truck. We knew of the danger ahead, but we also knew we had an even more powerful God. After a few pictures, we climbed aboard. As I got into the front seat, I could see that Henry—who had been in church the night before—wanted to talk, but we both knew it wasn't the right time.

Before long we were on the long, winding, uphill road to the refugee camps. It was the only road into the camps, and all along this dangerous roadway were places for the rebels to hide before launching their attacks. Being the only vehicle on the road, our truck was an inviting target carrying a lot of valuable things the rebels could use for themselves or sell to get money. I turned around and looked through the rear window of the truck; I could see the six soldiers, their weapons ready, vigilantly keeping a careful eye out for any threatening activity. Everyone was quiet. I kept on praying, *"Keep us safe, Lord. I remember Your promise to me, 'Do not be afraid, for I am with you wherever you go.' Even on this dangerous path, YOU ARE HERE, LORD!"* We were a big target, and I prayed that if any rebels were looking, their eyes would be blinded from seeing us. If God could make blind eyes see, He surely could make seeing eyes blind! After about half an hour of rugged driving, we finally saw the Pabbo camp. When we pulled up to the gates of the camp we let out a big sigh of relief, and the words *"Thank You, Jesus! Thank You, Lord!"* spontaneously came rushing out of my mouth.

Looking at the camp, all I could see for miles and miles was a sea of mud huts. The tiny huts were cramped closely together. Some of them had blue United Nations tarps draped over their thatched roofs, for the rebels were regularly shooting firebombs into the camps, destroying hundreds of huts. Also scattered throughout this sea of thatched-roof mud huts were many makeshift tents made out of wood, held together by blankets and people's clothing. These tents served as the refugees' only protection from the hot sun. Thousands upon thousands of people sat in the camp expressionless, almost motionless, surrounded by their meager possessions. I'd never seen such utter poverty in my entire life. It was much more dire and dreadful in person than what I'd seen in films or on television. I could feel myself starting to sink into despair for this mass of humanity. How could I possibly do this? I cried out to God, *"Lord, help me not to let my emotions get the best of me. Help me to stay focused."* We were taken into the headquarters of the camp and met with the camp director. After he shared with us some safety guidelines and a long list of dos and don'ts, we received his authorization to minister in the camp. With this, God had opened the final door!

Hundreds of people lined up to get water for the day in the Pabbo refugee camp.

Pastor Armstrong showed up ready to lead us over to his church, already full of people waiting for us. As we walked to the church in the stifling heat, my eyes scanned the camp. I saw a large tank; from it came a long pipe with a spigot at the end, delivering water. Hundreds of people of all ages were standing in a very long line, waiting for a turn to fill whatever vessel they had with precious water for the day. Already, the hot sun was beating down on them. Walking along, at first I found it hard to look at the incredibly blank and listless faces of so many people. I kept praying for a greater awareness of God's presence; and slowly, almost with each step I took, I felt joy and love rising up inside of me. I knew it wasn't me. In my own nature I just wanted to weep for them. The magnitude of all the pain, loss, thirst, hunger, and anguish was apparent everywhere I looked. But gradually, the Lord was helping me to look past all of that and to see these people with the loving eyes of Jesus. I could feel myself starting to smile and wave. Soon there was a whole trail of curious children following us to the church. Somewhere along the way, as we walked through the mazes of huts and swarms of people, we lost Kathy and Bob. Before long we reached the church—a large, unpretentious, windowless building with only one entrance. Once we were inside, the people sprang to their feet and began to cheer! Kathy and Bob had planned on teaching, with Pastor Armstrong as their interpreter. But now they were nowhere in sight. Since the crowd had been waiting for so long, Pastor Armstrong asked if I would share something with them. My heart leapt for joy, as once again the Lord was giving me an unexpected opportunity to teach the people of Africa!

I followed Pastor Armstrong to the front, where he motioned for me to stand next to him. I shot up a quick prayer, "*Help me, Lord!*" as I heard Pastor Armstrong tell his congregation that I was a teacher in America. While he was speaking, I noticed all of the restless children, and a song sprang into my mind. It was a simple, repetitive song about Jesus—a song with hand movements, easy enough for even these young children to learn and engage in. So, with Pastor Armstrong's help, we sang: "*Jesus! Jesus! Jesus in the morning, Jesus in the noontime. Jesus! Jesus! Jesus when the sun goes down.*" With each added verse, their singing became louder and louder; as they sang, they became more confident and full of feeling. They were having fun, and so was I.

It was a reminder to me that people—even children—are really the same all over the world.

Then I began to speak, stopping after each short phrase so that Pastor Armstrong could interpret what I said. With hundreds of refugees all jammed together, it was hot and humid in that closed-in space. Nevertheless, they listened attentively as I relayed God's message to them. Echoing what I had said the night before, I summoned them to "Thirst after Jesus and the Word of God." As Pastor Armstrong interpreted, I looked into the faces of the people. The few men I saw were old. I saw numerous pregnant women, many of them in that condition because of being raped by rebels and rogue soldiers. There were a lot of older women, a large number of young children, and many mothers nursing their babies. Some of these young mothers had a look of agony, with barely enough milk to keep their children alive. I knew they were in a desperate situation, and that Jesus could be their source of strength. I said, "We live in a fallen world and terrible things happen to you. But Jesus has not forgotten you. He says in His Word: *'Never will I leave you; never will I forsake you.' (Hebrews 13:5)* You don't have to listen to any of the lies of the enemy, the evil one. You can resist him and set your mind on Jesus. You don't have to be afraid. Even when you sleep, God doesn't sleep. He sends His angels to watch over you. He knows everything about you, and He still loves you."

I shared with them the words of Ephesians 3:16–19 and explained that this was my prayer for them: *"I pray that out of his glorious riches he may strengthen you with power through his Spirit in your inner being, so that Christ may dwell in your hearts through faith. And I pray that you, being rooted and established in love, may have power, together with all the saints, to grasp how wide and long and high and deep is the love of Christ, and to know this love that surpasses knowledge—that you may be filled to the measure of all the fullness of God."* I said, "God loves you and sent His Son, Jesus, for you. He invites you to come to Him. Come to Jesus, thank Him for saving you on the cross, and tell Him you love Him and trust Him. Come to Him exactly as you are."

Longing to see them encounter the eternal love of Jesus, I continued, "Raise your hand if you want to put your trust in Him!" Pastor Armstrong was interpreting excitedly in Swahili. Suddenly, many, many hands went up! Right then, Pastor Armstrong prayed in their language and they echoed him. It was beautiful sight. I said, "Just as you need water every day, you also need to thirst after God's Word. It will satisfy you, like drinking water does. Jesus will fill you with His abiding love, forgiveness, peace, and hope for your future. With God, all things are possible! Jesus is here for you! And you have a wonderful pastor here in this camp—Pastor Armstrong. He is here to teach you, to help you, and to pray for you." Afterwards, the Lord led me to move among the people gathered there and to pray for many of them. I was especially drawn to those who had sick children and to those who were dying of AIDS. I was able to touch them and to pray for them, even holding a baby in my arms. It truly was God's strength and grace that enabled me to do these things, and to do them without shedding a single tear!

Pastor Armstrong came over to me and said that he wanted to take me to where he lived in the camp, so that he could introduce me to his family. Little red clouds of dust swirled around me as I walked fast to keep up with his long legs. I tried to smile and wave at the people who were sitting in front of their huts, gazing at me in my very bright magenta outfit. Before long we arrived at Pastor Armstrong's small one-room mud hut. I bent over and followed him into the small opening of his home. He was smiling from ear to ear as he proudly introduced me to his nine children and his wife, Marilyn. I was humbled by the sheer poverty of their home, and yet amazed at the rich manners and character of their children, all of whom spoke very good English. Pastor Armstrong told me that he and Marilyn would be coming to a farewell dinner at the motel later that evening. I knew that would be my opportunity to give my sister's skirt to Marilyn.

Walking with Pastor Armstrong to his hut.

Now it was time for us to walk back to the gate so that we could drive over to the next refugee camp. It was quite a distance to get to the gate. As we went along, we gained a large entourage of people walking with us. I met a young man, in his early twenties, named Samuel. Walking together, I asked him to tell me about himself. I learned that rebels had killed his whole family, and he had almost died from a gunshot wound to his stomach. He pulled up his shirt to show me a big scar in the middle of his abdomen. Samuel had been in the camp church that morning when I was talking. He had heard what I said about God having a plan and purpose for our lives and about God never giving up on us. He told me that he knew the Lord had saved him for a reason, and he wanted to live his life for Jesus, telling other people in the camp about the Savior. Right then and there we stopped, held hands, and prayed together. I asked for the Holy Spirit to work mightily in Samuel's life, to guide him with His wisdom, and to give him help and direction so he could boldly speak out the Gospel of Jesus Christ. At that moment we both knew we had met each other for a bigger purpose—to encourage one another in living out the personal dream God had given to us. I look forward to seeing Samuel again in Heaven, and to meeting the many people from the camp who will be with him there, because his life was spared to be a witness for Jesus!

It was only a short drive to the smaller refugee camp of 30,000 people. When we arrived, a group of Africans lifted me up in the air and carried me on their hands, while squealing with joy, all the way to their church. I was asked to speak. And, once again, I saw the Spirit of God work in a wonderful way. Without a doubt this day in the refugee camps ended up being one of the most joyous and precious days of my life, sharing Jesus with people who needed Him. Not only that, God answered my prayer—miraculously, I had not shed one single tear!

Arriving safely back at the motel, we quickly freshened up and went down to a patio area where we would be sharing our final meal with our dear Ugandan pastors and their wives. Pastor Jacob and Margaret were there. As they promised, Pastor Armstrong and Marilyn were also there, and I was thrilled to be able to sit next to Marilyn. After I got to know more about her, she told me of her desire to reach out to women in the camp as a friend, to pray for them to know Christ as their Savior, and to teach them the Bible. I told her not every pastor's wife was like that, and she and her husband were a bright light to the people there. I loved hearing her stories of how God was using them to help meet the desperate needs of many people in the camp, and to bring thousands to eternal life in Christ. Surely, the Lord was working through Marilyn and Pastor Armstrong to create great good out of the great tragedy of the refugee camps.

After we finished eating, Kathy and Bob talked about how the Lord had worked during our time at the camps. We then gave to the pastors and their wives what was left in our plastic containers, so they could distribute it as they saw a need. I was pleased to give to Pastor Armstrong and Pastor Jacob several recordings of my husband's sermons, as well as players with batteries so they could listen to them as resources. To Margaret and Marilyn I gave prayer shawls that ladies from my church had knitted. Then, just as we were about to close with prayer, Pastor Jacob and Margaret asked me to come over to them. They spoke about how blessed they were by my sharing and teaching from the previous night, and that the people of the church wanted to give me a gift. They handed me a plastic bag. I opened the bag and pulled out a beautiful dress sewn by an Ugandan woman. It was purple! Tears spilled from my eyes as I slipped it over my head, right on top of my other clothes. The people of their church did not know all the things that had happened to me when I wore the purple skirt outfit back in Kenya, or how Mercy had given away her purple engagement dress. But God knew, and this beautiful gift would be a lasting reminder to me of all God had done during our time in Africa. Pastor Jacob said they had one more thing to give to me. They wanted to give me an African name! They said my new name was "Ife"—a Ugandan word, a name meaning "love." They both talked about how they could see the love of Jesus in me when I had talked in their church our first night in Gulu. I have received many gifts in the course of my life, but this gift of a new name was one of loveliest gifts I've ever received!

After sitting back down, I whispered to Marilyn that I needed a moment with her before they left. I briefly told her the story of the skirts and how, as I prayed, the Holy Spirit had prompted me to give away each skirt; that time and time again, He had held me back from giving away my sister Jan's skirt. When I met her quiet and humble husband the day before, I knew in my heart he must be married to an honorable and godly woman. And I was right! Looking Marilyn right in her eyes, I told her that I believed she was to receive my sister's skirt, not because it was anything fancy or expensive, but because it was a symbol of her faithfulness to pray and not give up. It was meant to honor her for being a prayer warrior and for her heart's desire to love lost people and share Jesus with them. God wanted to encourage her to not look at what she didn't have, but to look to the One who has everything—and who gave up everything—so that we could be with Him forever in Heaven. Whenever she wore this skirt, the Lord would be assuring her of the many blessings He has in store for those who pray, listen, and wait upon the Him. When I finished sharing my heart with Marilyn, I could see that she was slowly processing what I had told her. She wasn't accustomed to people being so personal with her, and she was deeply moved to know that the Lord had chosen her to receive this skirt. I could see that this dear sister, who loved so many others, at that moment felt very loved. Sensing the Lord's presence, we held each other's hands, grateful to God for His unfailing goodness and love.

Donna giving Marilyn the skirt from her sister, Jan.

The next morning we loaded our few remaining bags onto the back of the truck. Seeing Henry there, I told him I was looking forward to talking with him. He looked relieved. I knew he had been grappling with some things as he heard me speaking during our time in Gulu and the camps. Pastor Jacob and Pastor Armstrong were there, along with the two armed guards, as we joined hands once again for prayer. All of us realized the enormity of what had happened on this trip. From the depths of our hearts, we thanked the Lord for His faithfulness and presence in our lives, for bringing us together from across the ocean, and for His continued hand of love, blessing, and protection.

With that, we were on our way back to Kampala. Pastor Moses was sitting in the front, so I spent part of the trip praying for Henry and asking the Lord to give me some time to talk with him. When we reached the outskirts of Kampala, we stopped to drop Pastor Moses off near his home. We had been blessed to have him as our interpreter and guide. We all got out of the truck to meet his pretty and petite wife and their new baby. After a flurry of quick hugs and goodbyes, we hurried back to the truck, as we had to travel to the bus station in downtown Kampala. There we would catch a bus that would take us back to Nyahururu, Kenya.

I knew that this was my opportunity to talk with Henry. So I quickly climbed into the front seat of the truck, and we headed down the road. Henry began talking almost immediately, asking me questions about how he could really know for sure He was going to Heaven. *Wow!* I thought, *This is totally a "God-appointment!"* It was obvious to me that Henry had been listening a lot, and that the Holy Spirit had readied his heart. I asked him if he understood what sin meant. He shared with me about some of the bigger sins in his life. I could see that he was troubled when I reminded him that it took only one sin to separate us from a sinless God and a sinless Heaven forever.

By the time we got to the bus station, I knew I needed to find a quiet place to pray with Henry. And the Lord provided it. Kathy and Bob went off to buy the tickets while Henry and I sat outside on a bench. There, among the buses and crowds of people, I shared four important truths with Henry, asking him after each truth if he understood it:

1. God created you and all people. He loves you and has a marvelous plan for your life.

2. All people are sinful, and this sin separates us from God, so that we miss out on His best plan for our lives.

3. Because He loves us, God sent His Son, Jesus, to pay for our sins—yours and mine. On the cross, Jesus took our sins and

separation for us, so that we could be forgiven and be with God forever. He rose from the dead, and He now offers to you and all people a new life today—and eternal life in Heaven—as a free gift.

4. We receive this life-changing gift when God's Holy Spirit leads us to trust in Jesus to be our Savior, and not in anything we ourselves have done.

I asked Henry if he wanted to pray and receive God's gift of salvation for him by trusting in Jesus. Without hesitation, he said, "Yes!" We joined hands and he repeated a simple prayer, a phrase at a time. It was a prayer similar to this: *"Dear Lord, I am a sinner and I am sorry for my sins. Please forgive me. I believe You died on the cross for me. Thank You for the gift of Heaven. Thank You for hearing and answering my prayer. In Jesus' name, Amen."* Then, with great joy, I shared with Henry the promise from 1 John 5:13: *"I write these things to you who believe in the name of the Son of God so that you may know that you have eternal life."*

Lastly, I gave Henry a little New Testament Bible I had been carrying in my purse. I reminded him that he needed to read God's Word every day. Because Henry had been talking about how I used the water and the sponge in church, I encouraged him to "be like a sponge and fill up on Jesus" every day. He quickly nodded his head. Just then, Kathy and Bob walked up with our tickets. The bus to Nyahururu was ready to leave, and we had to get on board before we lost our seats. I gave Henry a hug. We had spent three amazing days with one other. Together we had seen Jesus' love not only touching thousands of lives in the impoverished refugee camps, but also touching the needy life of a young driver in a major general's truck. It was hard to say good-bye, but because of what Jesus had done, we had the hope of heaven and we both knew we would see each other again!

If you want to pray, listen, and respond to God...
Have a passionate desire to see people come to know the
eternal love of Jesus Christ.

CHAPTER SEVEN - REFLECTION PAGES

"Have a passionate desire to see people come to know the eternal love of Jesus Christ."

PRAY AND LISTEN TO GOD AS YOU READ THESE WORDS FROM THE BIBLE

Isaiah 60:1–3
Arise, shine, for your light has come, and the glory of the Lord rises upon you. See, darkness covers the earth and thick darkness is over the peoples, but the the LORD rises upon you and his glory appears over you. Nations will come to your light, and kings to the brightness of your dawn.

Luke 19:10
For the Son on Man came to seek and to save what was lost.

Luke 15:4–7
Suppose one of you has a hundred sheep and loses one of them. Does he not leave the ninety-nine in the open country and go after the lost sheep until he finds it? And when he finds it, he joyfully puts it on his shoulders and goes home. Then he calls his friends and neighbors together and says, "Rejoice with me; I have found my lost sheep." I tell you that in the same way there will be more rejoicing in heaven over one sinner who repents than over ninety-nine righteous persons who do not need to repent."

Acts 20:24
However, I consider my life worth nothing to me, if only I may finish the race and complete the task the Lord has given me—the task of testifying to the gospel of God's grace.

John 7:37–38
If anyone is thirsty, let him come to me and drink. Whoever believes in me, as the Scripture has said, streams of living water will flow from within him.

Isaiah 58:11
The LORD will guide you always; he will satisfy your needs in a
sun-scorched land and will strengthen your frame. You will be like
a well-watered garden, like a spring whose waters never fail.

Philemon 6
I pray that you may be active in sharing your faith, so that you will
have a full understanding of every good thing we have in Christ.

QUESTIONS FOR REFLECTION AND DISCUSSION

1. What do the refugee camps in this skirt story show us about the condition of our world today?

2. Look at the story Jesus told about the woman with the lost coin in Luke 15:8–10 in your Bible. In what specific ways were Donna, Marilyn, and Samuel like the woman in this passage?

3. What difference do you think people coming to know Jesus and His love would have made in the refugee camps? What difference would it make in your family and community?

4. What does praying, listening, and responding to God have to do with telling other people about Jesus?

5. Tell about a time you told someone about Jesus. What were some of your feelings?

6. In what specific ways did God open doors—and take care of the details—for Donna to share the love of Jesus in the refugee camps? What doors do you see Him opening in your life for you to share Jesus with someone?

7. What is one step of faith that you are going to pray about taking as a result of your time reading and reflecting on this skirt story?

PRAYER OF RESPONSE

Lord of the Harvest, I praise You for Your passionate desire to see people come to know You and Your salvation. Thank You that this desire led You all that way to a cross, and then led You to seek me and find me. Stir up this same desire in me to go wherever You want me to go and do whatever You want me to do, to share Your eternal love with others. There are so many people who need to know You—the harvest is waiting! As I continue to grow in praying, listening, and responding to you, may I become more active in sharing my faith. I ask You to shine Your light through me to those in my family, community, and the world who are living in darkness. Let me be a channel for Your living water. By the power of Your Holy Spirit, help me take specific steps of faith so that I will be like the woman who persistently searched for her lost coin. And, in turn, may I come to a fuller understanding of every good thing I have in You. In your saving name I pray, Amen!

SKIRT STORY NUMBER SEVEN— NANCY AND ESTHER

*If you want to pray, listen and respond to God...
Join together with others in praying, listening, and
responding to God.*

With my ticket in hand, I grabbed ahold of the bar to pull myself up into the bus headed to Kenya. Kathy and Bob were fortunate to find two seats side by side; and I was relieved to locate a vacant window seat next to an older woman. Still overwhelmed from what had just happened with Henry, I needed some quiet time to think. *Lord,* I prayed, *You did this amazing thing in Henry's life! He was in darkness, but now he is in the light. Now he is a new creation! Thank You for the countless numbers of things that You did in this past week, including giving me time with Henry. Being privileged to witness his spiritual birth into a new life in Christ was downright incredible!*

As our bus started up and slowly pulled out of the station, I began to feel unsettled. For me, watching Henry give his life to Jesus—and then having to leave him so quickly—was like witnessing the joy of a new baby being born and then walking away, leaving it on its own. I felt anxious, and I knew my anxiety was rooted in fear. I had to deal with these fears right away; I had to refocus my mind on remembering God's Word and all the amazing things He had done. Surely it was no surprise to God that Henry's spiritual birth had happened when and where it did. I could rest in His promise to work much good in and through all things. The thought came into my mind that I couldn't be there with Henry, but the Holy Spirit was there! I said, *"Thank you for that comforting thought, Lord."* I began to feel God's perfect love pushing out my fear.

I knew at that moment Henry was driving home to his family in Kampala. So I began praying for him. My prayer went something like this: *"Help me to let go of my fears. All I can do is to turn them over to You. Strengthen Henry, Lord. You prompted me to urge him to tell his wife all that happened in the past week leading up to his prayer of faith today. Help him to do that right away. Guard and protect his newborn faith from any doubts and assaults of the enemy, whom I know wants to lie, steal, or even kill that seed of faith. Instill in Henry a daily desire to read Your Word. Remind him of the 'sponge' story. Lead him and his wife to read the Bible together. Bring someone to come alongside of him, to water that seed of faith, and to help him stay connected to Your Word. Thank You for what You did in this young man. Help him to join together with other believers in using his life as a living testimony to You, Jesus!"*

As I thought and prayed, my heart gradually began to calm down. I started to experience that peace that passes all understanding. But, all at once, loud, blaring music came crackling through the sound system of the bus, interrupting my peaceful conversation with God. After our days in the major general's truck, I'd forgotten how noisy and chaotic bus rides in Africa could be! This twelve-hour journey to Kenya was going to be a long one.

My mind was whirling from all that had transpired over the past few days. I had been in a hurricane of once-in-a-lifetime experiences. Wanting to write it all down, I pulled a notebook out of my bag. But I just sat there, pen in hand, unable to record anything. So I gazed numbly out the window, watching the locals as the bus passed through the stark poverty of the slum areas on the outskirts of Kampala. Children were digging through trash heaps, looking for scraps of food or items to sell. Others were filling up vessels with murky-looking water from small streams. Watching people biking and walking down the streets, some balancing burdens on their heads, I prayed my simple prayer, *"Help me not to forget them, Lord."*

Before long, we were out of the city and traveling through the countryside. I took out my camera, knowing we'd be leaving Uganda soon. I snapped away, wanting to record as much as I could. Groves of banana trees, fig trees, mango, and papaya trees grew along the roadway and hills. Like a painting on canvas, the landscape looked so picturesque with beautiful tropical flowers and bougainvillea vines of orange, white, pink and magenta-colored blossoms.

Also dotting the countryside were all different sizes and shapes of anthills. Amazingly, some of these anthills were at least twenty feet tall. Having taught many school lessons through the years on how hard ants work, I tried to take as many pictures as I could of these astonishing architectural monuments built by such tiny creations of the Lord. I was happy to be in a window seat so I could take better pictures. Somehow, this diversion of picture taking helped to calm down my mind, and I was gradually sensing more and more of God's peace. So I just kept clicking away.

After passing through a sudden thunderstorm, I was blessed to capture a picture of a huge rainbow breaking through the clouds and stretching majestically across the landscape of Uganda. It was spectacular! Although we had quite a bit of rain at various times in the past weeks, I'd never seen a rainbow during my time in Africa. Believing that the Lord speaks to us through His creation, and that he wants us to be open to his signs, I asked, *Why did this happen now? What does this mean?* At that moment, my mind went back to Noah in the Bible and the message of hope and assurance God gave him through a rainbow. I found myself quietly praying, *How like You, Lord, to send such a timely and beautiful reminder of Your ever-faithful presence and the promises of Your Word. Yes, You are with us wherever we go! Now I can let go of anxiety about leaving Henry. He is safe in the hands of Jesus!*

The hours went by slowly as our bus stopped many times—at the border crossing between Uganda and Kenya, gas stations, barricades, checkpoints, and bus stops along the way. Every time we stopped at military checkpoints, soldiers armed with weapons would come aboard our bus, searching passengers and demanding that we produce our passports and visas. I kept praying, asking the Holy Spirit to set my mind on the promises of God's care for us, and not on my fear of being taken off the bus and detained somewhere. And, although night had fallen, I found it impossible to sleep with the continual bumping of the bus over uneven roads, music blaring, people talking in their fast-paced language, babies crying, children running up and down the aisle, and animals barking or bleating loudly. After many hours, the bus driver finally announced our stop! We had arrived at our destination on the outskirts of Nyahururu, Kenya. It was 3:30 a.m. in the morning. Gathering our stuff, we followed the driver, moving carefully down the steps into the chilly morning air. Making our way through the darkness, we retrieved our few bags out of the storage area from underneath the bus.

As the bus pulled away, we saw them. Standing there with big smiles, shivering from the cold, were two wonderful African women. They were our friends, Nancy and Esther. We had met these two loving and compassionate women when we were last in Nyahururu, three weeks before. We were hoping that Pastor Moses had been able to reach them by phone from Kampala, asking them to pick us up at the bus station. Thankfully they had gotten the message and had arrived just as our bus was driving away. Seeing Nancy and Esther standing there, I thought, *Lord, they are such a wonderful pair You've brought together for Your purposes.* Both were widowed and were grandmothers. Nancy was a tall, attractive businesswoman. Esther, shorter in stature, was an always helpful behind-the-scenes, get-it-done kind of person. Working together, they had a thriving ministry to help women in Nyahururu. They were a team. Now here they came, dashing towards us, still smiling from ear to ear. How good it was to see them! We hugged one another and quickly loaded our few remaining bags into Nancy and Esther's small cars.

It was a short drive to Nancy's apartment. When we arrived, it was very evident to Nancy and Esther that we all needed to sleep.

Bob and Kathy made their way to the bed in Nancy's room, while I collapsed on a small couch, still wanting to talk to these "old friends." Nancy and Esther sat down in chairs next to me. I dropped off almost immediately into a deep sleep. A few hours later I awoke; I knew I was exhausted, because I hadn't even heard the wail of the horn at daybreak. Upon opening my eyes, I saw Nancy and Esther's smiling faces. Nancy whispered, "You were talking, and then you weren't." Ha! Ha! Ha!

They both motioned for me to tiptoe into the kitchen, so as not to wake Bob and Kathy. Nancy poured us a cup of hot chai, which is the Swahili word for tea. Chai is simply a kind of tea mixed with milk and sugar. The warm cup felt good as I wrapped my fingers around it and settled down at Nancy's small table. I felt as though I'd known these two sweet sisters in Christ my entire life. We leaned in toward each other almost giddy, sipping chai like girlfriends catching up and sharing stories. They could hardly wait to hear all that had happened in the weeks since we left Nyahururu for Mombasa. They recalled what a shock it was when Barbara learned that her mother had died, and how hard it was for all of us when she had to leave so quickly to return to America.

As we sat together in Nancy's kitchen, my mind drifted back to some of those first days in Africa. Could it have been only a little over three weeks ago that I had first met Nancy and Esther? It seemed like months had passed since my first Saturday in Nyahururu....

On that Saturday three weeks before, Barbara and I were at the site of a large graduation ceremony. This ceremony was for African nationals who had taken classes for two years to become pastors or Bible teachers. Hundreds of graduates, along with their families and friends, had gathered there. The Holy Spirit arranged things so that Barbara and I met Nancy and Esther. Because we were clueless about how to navigate the newness of our surroundings, they lovingly took us under their wings.

After finding a quiet place to talk, the four of us bonded almost immediately. We learned that Nancy and Esther were both widows. Not only did they have that in common, they also shared a similar desire to help women of all ages—especially widows, single mothers, and others who were alone and in need. They believed that the Lord had called them to give these women some of the necessary tools to survive by training them and showing them ways to provide for themselves and their families.

Nancy and Esther had teamed together to bring needy women into their two small homes for workshops designed to teach them different skills. In addition, these two sisters in Christ were also conducting weekly Bible studies and prayer times, thereby helping needy women to discover their true worth and identity in Jesus Christ. And for some of the women in more desperate circumstances, Nancy and Esther would even provide them with a place to live until they could make it on their own. In spite of their own personal losses, these two widows had found a way to serve the Lord together in a new capacity. Barbara and I were thrilled to talk with them! And, before the conference was over late that afternoon, Nancy and Esther excitedly informed us they had made arrangements with their pastor for both of us to speak at their church the next morning.

Now, three weeks later, I sat in Nancy's apartment and listened to Nancy and Esther as they chatted away. Enjoying my chai, I pictured in my mind's eye that first Sunday morning when we had spoken in their church....

That morning, Barbara and I had been seated in the front of the church on a small platform. When the band started playing, the whole place erupted as everyone jumped to their feet. It was as though the entire building was swaying from side to side, filled with the energy and enthusiasm of people singing and dancing in worship to the Lord. Wanting to worship with them, we tried singing and clapping as best as we could, even though we didn't know the songs. Their worship was definitely the kind that was a vigorous "full body" worship, with a lot of rhythm and physical movement. Even though it was strenuous and I was sweaty from head to toe, I still loved it! Culturally, it was very different from what we were used to. But we weren't expecting it to be the same as what we were familiar with. We simply felt it was a privilege to be joining with them in their way of worship as they expressed their heartfelt love and praise to the Lord.

After our time of singing, the pastor of the church—Pastor Walter—read from the Bible and shared a teaching from God's Word. Then he introduced Barbara. As she spoke, there was a sparkle in her eyes and a wonderful radiance in her countenance. The Holy Spirit was obviously enabling Barbara to share her heart for Jesus and the people of Africa. The congregation was noticeably touched by her love. They responded throughout her talk by waving their hands, shouting "Hallelujah!" and "Amen!" and squealing loudly. Little did we know that this would be Barbara's only opportunity to speak in a church while she was in Africa.

Then, with Nancy serving as my interpreter, I spoke next. Standing on the platform wearing my sister Jan's skirt, I saw an eager look on the beautiful faces of the people. I'm sure they were probably wondering how and why these two middle-aged women—the only non-African women present there that morning—had shown up quite unexpectedly in their church. In my mind I prayed, *This is it—my first time to share in Africa! Help me, Holy Spirit, to be Your mouthpiece, to teach what is acceptable to You and bring to them what they need to hear.* I told the church who I was, where I was from, and how I'd ended up there. I shared with them how unlikely it would have been for me to make it to Africa by myself, but the Lord had made it possible when he teamed me together with Barbara. I also assured them that, just as He was working in our lives, He was working in their lives, too. I talked about how Jesus is always working through the circumstances of people's lives in ways we don't even know about, to allow us to do things we normally wouldn't be able to do.

As I spoke, I could sense the power of the Lord come over me. Barbara and I had been told that this was a church with many believers, but they needed encouragement to reach out to their unbelieving neighbors and friends. For the first time in Africa, I opened my Bible and read Jesus' last words to his disciples in Matthew 28:19–20: *"Therefore go and make disciples of all nations, baptizing them in the name of the Father and of the Son and of the Holy Spirit, and teaching them to obey everything I have commanded you. And surely I am with you always, to the very end of the age."*

After reading this Scripture, I explained: "Jesus said 'GO!' to His disciples. These words were a command, not a suggestion. And they were for all of God's people—people of all ages, from all nations and continents—not just for His disciples standing around Him right before He returned to Heaven. These words are meant for YOU—not just pastors, teachers, missionaries, or people like Barbara and me from America. The Bible tells all believers in Jesus to 'go and make disciples.'" Then, out of my mouth, came these words: "I think the Lord is stirring in someone's heart, right now, to go. As the Lord brought us here to teach people in Africa, I believe that some African who is present here today will be going to America to teach about Jesus!"

I went on to say, "Earlier this morning when I was getting dressed, a thought came into my mind. The thought was that I should wear a 'fish' necklace someone gave me a long time ago. And here it is—can you see it? It's this heavy, clunky, fish-shaped thing made from clay that is hanging around my neck. When I wear it, it reminds me that I am to catch 'fish.' By that I don't mean that I should get a fishing pole and go fishing in the river. Instead, this necklace is a reminder for me to be like Jesus by being a fisher of men. Jesus said in Mark 1:17, *'Come, follow me, and I will make you fishers of men.'* What He meant is that there are people all around us who are not believers; they do not yet believe, or trust, in Jesus as their Savior. And Jesus tells us who know Him, *'When you know, you must go!'* You must go and tell the good news of Jesus to 'fish'—to lost people—starting with those right around you! It is not up to you whether they receive Him or reject Him. That's the Holy Spirit's job to bring them to faith. Our job is to simply go and lovingly tell them about Jesus. He will do the rest."

Pointing to the necklace hanging around my neck, I said, "Just like this necklace is a little heavy and uncomfortable for me to wear, it can also be uncomfortable to talk to someone about Jesus. It can be scary, just as it is scary for me to stand up and speak to you right now. But Jesus said, *'Surely I am with you always.'* (Matthew 28:20)

You are not alone. Jesus sent His Holy Spirit to help. It's His Spirit who enables me to do this. As I am speaking to you, Jesus is helping me. And He will also help you to tell others about Him. Many times I have said these words, *'What You say, Lord, I will do!'* I want you to say those words right now." As one, the people in the church responded: *"What You say, Lord, I will do!"* Then I said, "Say it again, but louder!" And they did, shouting, *"What You say, Lord, I will do!"* It was awesome to hear their response!

I closed by teaching them a song entitled "I Will Make You Fishers of Men, If You Follow Me." It was a simple song that I knew everyone, even the children, could sing. They all sang the song with Spirit-given enthusiasm, committing themselves to being fishers of men for Jesus. Then I closed with a prayer, having them repeat after me a phrase at a time: *"Lord Jesus, Thank You for loving me and saving me. Thank You for helping me to be a fisher of men. Lead me to people who need to know You. Help me to not be afraid and to GO as you commanded me. Remind me that You are with me always. In Your name, Amen."*

When I sat back down, Pastor Walter came up and asked the people if any of them had anything to say. One young man stood up and said when I had talked about God's Spirit stirring in someone's heart, he immediately knew he was the one. He explained that even before I had said it, he sensed in his heart the Lord was telling him he was to go—go to America and teach. He knew he was to be a fisher of men! His eyes were wet with tears but also dancing with joy. For him this was a confirmation from the Holy Spirit, giving him a dream and a vision for his future. At that moment I couldn't help but think of the dream God had given me as a child, and how He had brought that dream to fulfillment.

Nancy poured more chai into our cups and we sipped our tea, still feeling the emotions of that Sunday. Our conversation continued as we recalled the amazing thing that happened next....

At the end of the service, Pastor Walter invited Barbara and me to come back on the platform and pray for people. We stood side by side watching as people started lining up for prayer. *Oh, my,* I thought, *I need Your help here, Lord!* The very first one to come to me for prayer was a strikingly beautiful young woman accompanied by her mother. I asked, "How can I pray for you?" The young woman was obviously embarrassed to talk about what was wrong. Her mother spoke for her, telling me that her daughter had a large goiter on the side of her neck. She had been afflicted with it for a long, long time, and it just kept getting bigger and bigger. I saw it, and it was huge. I thought, *Well, nothing is too difficult for You, God.* Looking into the young woman's eyes, I asked her if she believed in Jesus and had faith He could heal her. She nodded her head. Then, after getting her permission to lay my fingers on her neck, I prayed. I thanked Jesus for loving her, for giving her the courage to come up for prayer and for trusting Him to take the goiter away. As I was praying for her healing in the name of Jesus, something was happening under my fingers. That huge goiter slowly shrank away to nothing! I had never experienced anything like it before! The three of us stood there stunned, gradually taking in what the Lord had done. It was a miracle and we knew it! Warm tears started running down our faces. We huddled close together, thanking Jesus for what He had done. What happened next reminded me of the man who, after he had been healed at the entrance to the temple, went *"walking and jumping, and praising God."* (Acts 3:8) I watched as this mother and her daughter, rejoicing and praising God with loud African squeals, literally went dancing out of the church. I prayed, *"Use this, Lord, to bring others to You."* To this day I wish I could have heard them telling others the story of what God had done!

Over the next hour many more people came forward for prayer. I would pause each time before I prayed, asking the Holy Spirit what I should pray for and what Scriptures He wanted me to speak out. Then I would sense His presence gently washing over me, and a verse from God's Word would often come into my mind. I would share Scriptures like some of these: *"But seek first his kingdom and his right-eousness, and all these things will be given to you as well."* (Matthew 6:33); *"Peace I leave with you; my peace I give to you. I do not give to you as the world gives. Do not let your hearts be troubled and do not be afraid."* (John 14:27) *"'For I know the plans I have for you,' declares the LORD, 'plans to prosper you and not to harm you, plans to give you hope and a future. Then you will call on me and come and pray to me, and I will listen to you. You will seek me and find me when you seek me with all your heart.'"* (Jeremiah 29:11–13) I had learned if you spend time reading and memorizing God's Word, the Holy Spirit will bring it to your remembrance while you are praying. And God faithfully works through His Word to heal, bless, and encourage. That morning I could see Him using the sum total of who He was in me through all the days of my life. Even though I was scared, tired and weak, I was a willing vessel. Yes, there are times we don't always "hear" right. But He always knows the intent of our hearts, and He brings good even out of our mistakes. We can trust Him! As 2 Peter 1:3 says: *"His divine power has given us everything we need for life and godliness through our knowledge of him who called us by his own glory and goodness."*

At this point in our conversation around Nancy's small kitchen table, Esther laughed and said her grandkids were still talking about my clunky fish necklace and were still singing the "Fishers of Men" song. Her words were an encouraging reminder to me of the blessings that come when we listen to God, even when He asks us to wear things like a clunky fish necklace. Hearing what Esther shared made me want to be even more attentive to what Jesus wants to do in and through me. He is the great *"I AM!"* (John 18:5) He is Lord of the present tense—always right there with us, wherever we are, working to make us "fishers of men." I could see this in my life, and I certainly could see this in the lives of Nancy and Esther—two beautiful sisters in Christ who were serving Him together as one!

I sat there tired but happy, listening to both of them excitedly talking away about the Lord and what He was doing in their lives and in the lives of young women they were reaching for Jesus. Nancy and Esther didn't know it, but the Holy Spirit had already shown me that I was to give each of them a skirt outfit. These would be the final skirts I had to give away. I smiled, thinking about my secret—the secret of the skirts. I could hardly contain my excitement. I wanted to give them the skirts right away, but I had learned, through the giving of skirts over the past few weeks, the importance of prayerfully waiting for the Lord to show me just the right time. I didn't want to run ahead of Him. He'd been so faithful in leading me thus far.

How fitting it was that as I was thinking about the skirts, Nancy and Esther were telling me about some of the things they had recently acquired to train women with new skills. They'd obtained several wooden contraptions that looked much like spinning wheels from the early colonial days in America. These devices were used for weaving cloth. Nancy and Esther had taught themselves how to use them. They, in turn, were training women how to weave. Many of these women had husbands and children who had died of AIDS. They desperately needed help, and they were getting it.

Esther, on the left, and Nancy, on the right, with one of their weaving machines.

Here were Nancy and Esther, God's servants, working together to make a difference in the lives of poverty-stricken women and children. These two African widows, who had so little themselves, were giving so much. They both knew that they could accomplish more for the

Lord together than they could ever accomplish separately. Every day they denied things for themselves so that they could supply food, medicine, and other essentials to many hurting women and children. Nancy and Esther's lives were a visible demonstration to me of the two great commandments Jesus talked about: *"Love the Lord your God with all your heart and with all your soul and with all your mind.' This is the first and greatest commandment. And the second is like it: 'Love your neighbor as yourself.'"* (Matthew 22:37–39) Blessed are those who hear the word of God and do it! They were doing it!

When there was a pause in our conversation, I knew it was time for me to give the skirts to Nancy and Esther. I opened my bag and pulled out a plastic sack containing the last two sets of skirts. I told them how the Lord had led me to give away numerous skirts to women over the past several weeks. When I shared with Nancy and Esther how I had first started praying and waiting on the Lord to show me why, when, and to whom I should give the skirts, they were almost beside themselves. They really wanted to see and learn more about the skirts God had set aside for them.

The first one I pulled out was the magenta-colored skirt and jacket outfit. I presented it to Nancy. I shared with her that it was Barbara's skirt which she had planned to wear in the refugee camps in Uganda, and how I had worn it in her place to honor her. I explained that I personally would not have chosen to wear such a loud, brightly-colored outfit, but I discovered that it was exactly what I was supposed to wear. I had prayed for the Lord to be my joy and strength that day in the refugee camps, to sustain me physically and emotionally, and to help me not to cry. I described to Nancy how God had intervened, enabling me to have unspeakable joy and to be loving and encouraging to people in the camps. That day as I wore this skirt and jacket outfit, I had been clothed with the power and promise of God that *"the joy of the LORD is your strength."* (Nehemiah 8:10)

I looked at Nancy and said, "Just as this skirt and jacket are a bright, happy color, I know that when you wear it you, too, will bring the joy and happiness of the Lord to others. It will be a symbol of the Spirit's power, love, and presence shining through you." Nancy, thrilled to know it was Barbara's skirt, grabbed it out of my hands and went right into another room to put it on. When she came back into the kitchen, she was twirling around and around with a big smile, definitely radiating the joy of the Lord! She looked stunning! It was a perfect fit, and I could tell she liked it. After all, many women and girls—no matter their age or nationality—like a skirt that twirls! I thought how blessed Barbara would be to see the look on Nancy's face as she was spinning around!

Beaming and excited, Nancy sat down. Now the time had arrived for me to give away my last skirt. It was the skirt the Lord had me save just for Esther. I still remember how Esther had driven Barbara and me in her tiny old car, its tired and worn shocks having given out years before. Together we'd bumped up and down the muddy one-lane roads on the way to her church our first Sunday in Africa, and then again to the orphanage the next day after we found out Barbara's mother had died. Esther was present—always praying, always willing, always ready to help. She was such a servant, making herself available regardless of her circumstances and means. The skirt God had set aside for Esther had been given by Connie, a humble intercessory prayer warrior who was also a widow. Like Esther, she did not like to be in the spotlight. She preferred to stay behind the scenes humbly praying, working hard, and serving Jesus. Connie's skirt was full of brightly colored flowers and was paired with a green jacket. Esther tried it on, and it fit her so well. I looked at the predominately green color in the skirt and jacket. Green is the color for growth, and I knew that both of these skirts would bring growth and encouragement to Nancy and Esther as they served the Lord together as one. These outfits would be a boost to them—a sign from the Lord that He was taking care of every single detail of their lives!

Realizing what God had done through these simple skirts, the three of us prayed together. We thanked the Lord for Barbara and Connie who, like Nancy and Esther, were also widows committed to loving and helping others. We asked Him to bless these skirts so they would be symbols of His love, provision, and guidance, as Esther and

Nancy served Jesus in all their endeavors. We huddled in Nancy's little kitchen, quiet and speechless for a moment, thinking about the significance of it all. The presence of the Lord enveloped us as we stood together, our arms around each other's shoulders. We were experiencing what Jesus promised in Matthew 18:20: *"For where two or three come together in my name, there I am with them."* It was a time that none of us wanted to end.

But the clock was ticking! Bob, Kathy, and I had a long drive ahead of us to get to the airport in Nairobi for our flight back to America. Depending on the road, the condition of our taxi, checkpoints, and other unforeseen circumstances, it could easily take five to eight hours of driving time to get there. Nancy and Esther drove us over to Pastor Weston and Violet's house, where a taxi-van would pick us up and take us to the airport. Upon our arrival at their home the metal gate opened, and out ran Sheba and Sammy. It was wonderful to see their happy, familiar faces. With an interesting sparkle in their eyes, they practically lifted me up and carried me into the house.

When I stepped inside, Violet and Weston were standing there, smiling and holding a box. They handed it to me, saying it was a "love gift" symbolizing all the love I had given to them and had also shared in their nation. Surprised and overwhelmed, I hugged Violet, thanking them both for their gift. When I opened the box, I couldn't believe it. Overcome with emotion, I carefully pulled out of the box a beautiful purple and silver dress, complete with a head wrap! It was the kind of dress an African woman would wear for special celebrations—very traditional and fancy. I was shocked. There was no way Pastor Weston and Violet could have known about all the events that had taken place while I was wearing Ann's purple skirt in Mombassa. And they wouldn't have known how the Lord kept me from giving that purple skirt away until I gave it to Mercy in Kampala. And, of course, they weren't aware of the story of Mercy giving away her priceless, purple engagement dress for an unknown woman in the refugee camps. At that moment I knew God's Spirit was bringing to me a great blessing through this act of kindness from Pastor Weston and Violet. They didn't know all that had happened to me with the skirts, and they were totally clueless as to the "bigger picture" meaning of this moment for me. But they were willing to act when the Lord impressed them to do this. It was a reminder to me that when we pray, listen, and then respond to a leading from God, we may not even know or understand why we are doing it other than we believe God is telling us to do it. But in that act of faith, we are being used by the Lord to fulfill a "bigger picture" moment in our lives and in the lives of others.

As I held the dress in my arms, I could see that they wanted me to try it on. So that's what I did. Violet took me by the hand, led me into her and Pastor Weston's room, and helped me put on that beautiful silvery purple dress. I felt like I was getting ready for a big event! At that moment, Violet and I were like good friends—laughing, talking, quickly catching up on how things were going at the orphanage. She lovingly showed me how to fold the head wrap around my head. I was full to overflowing by her expression of love and kindness as we walked back out hand in hand. Although the dress was a little on the big side, everyone clapped when they saw me. The fit didn't matter, not one iota! What mattered was what the dress stood for— our oneness in the love of Jesus, and our joy in all that He had done! We smiled as pictures were snapped. Then I had to quickly change, as we knew that our ride to the airport would be arriving soon. When I got back to the room, Pastor Weston and Violet gathered us all in one big circle. Together we called out to the Lord in prayer, humbly thanking Him for doing more than we had asked for or had even imagined. When we were finished we hovered close to each other, realizing the magnitude of these last minutes together.

Violet with Donna as she wears the traditional
silvery purple dress.

The blaring horn of the taxi-van broke the intensity of the moment. Everyone helped us to gather up our remaining bags and followed us to the waiting taxi parked outside the gate. After putting our things aboard, we had just a short time to say our final goodbyes. Knowing it was my last opportunity, I asked the Holy Spirit to give me a word of blessing or encouragement that I could quietly whisper in each person's ear as we hugged for the last time. Then the moment arrived to climb aboard, find our seats, and start our final journey to the airport. As the taxi pulled away, I looked back once more—they were all standing at the big metal gate, watching us. The Lord had blessed and honored the desires of my heart through each person standing there. With a heavy heart, I waved. They waved back. Then the tears came. I was glad that I was sitting all alone in the backseat of the van.

Grateful for the solitude, I began gazing out the window at the beautiful Kenyan countryside. I was still amazed to see zebras and monkeys near the roadside as we drove along. About halfway to Nairobi, the driver stopped at a "roadside cafe"—a loose translation for a shack with a fire out front where food was being cooked over an open flame. We didn't stay there long, and soon we were back on the road. Nightfall was approaching, and I could barely see the people walking along the roadside under the dimly lit sky. I once again quietly prayed, *"Protect them, Lord."* And, when we drove through the slum districts on the outskirts of town, I knew these would be my last glimpses of Africa. *"Help me not to forget them, Lord."*

In the gathering dusk, our taxi pulled into a busy lane of traffic in front of the airport. Upon stopping at the "Departing Nairobi" sign, the driver pulled out our bags and pointed us to the correct door into the terminal. After getting our tickets and going through all the checkpoints and inspections, we made our way to the gate from which we'd catch our flight to Amsterdam. Because we had several hours before our plane departed, we went walking for a brief time through the tourist shops in the area near our gate. Still overwhelmed from what I had seen in the refugee camps and all that had happened in the past four weeks, I had no desire to buy any of the last-minute souvenirs that were being sold there—sadly, many of the souvenirs were actually made in China.

Eventually, Kathy, Bob, and I found some seats, sat down, and started to talk. We knew that, quite possibly, this might well be our last opportunity to be together. So we reminisced. We had shared many times and experiences with one other. We laughed as we recalled the day trip we took to the animal park with the eighth graders from

Violet's orphanage. Many of these orphans had never seen the animals of their own country. We chuckled, remembering how each one of us patted an old sedated rhino, played with monkeys, fed long-necked giraffes, and quickly ran when hippos suddenly popped their heads up out of a stream right by where we were standing!

Then we began to talk about deeper matters, and the heartbreak and uncertainty that had come with the death of Barbara's mother. Everything had changed upon Barbara's sudden departure. We choked back tears, remembering how the Lord brought good from it all. My childhood dream of teaching children in Africa had been fulfilled, and not only once but many times over. We marveled at how God brought young James across my path by the outhouse that Sunday morning in Mombassa; we laughed as we remembered how James and I had looked marching around that church seven times.

We knowingly acknowledged that we had made mistakes along the way and could have done some things better. But over and over again we had seen God honor His promise in Romans 8:28: *"And we know that in all things God works for the good of those who love him, who have been called according to his purpose."* We had certainly witnessed that in Mombassa when I first held back from giving to the Lord what He wanted me to give, and how He subsequently brought great good for the church as the people began to listen and obey. Not only had the Lord provided them with more than a year's worth of ministry funds that day, He also had faithfully provided for us everything that we needed for the rest of our days in Africa!

We talked about how blessed we were to speak at the dedication of the newly completed church building in the Congo, after its destruction from the erupting volcano. I knew I would never forget Jean who had given up her comfortable life in America to serve the young women of Kigali—and how she had been wanting sheets for her bed, and the Lord worked it out so that I still had Barbara's brand-new sheets to give to her. She was a great example of God's promise in Psalm 37:4: *"Delight yourself in the LORD and he will give you the desires of your heart."*

Filled with gratitude and amazement at God's care and protection, we recalled what He had done during our time in Uganda. The Lord had opened the door for us to broadcast on the radio, not once but twice. He had brought Rose's husband, the colonel, to faith in Jesus. He had used the colonel to give us a "sitting" with the major general. He had led the major general to give us his official truck and armed guards for our time in the refugee camps. No doubt, the Lord had moved the hearts of people in high places to provide life-saving coverage for us. *"Before they call I will answer; while they are still speaking I will hear."* (Isaiah 65:24)

The greatest highlights, of course, were the prayers of people who prayed for salvation, assurance, provision, reconciliation and healing, as God's Spirit worked faith in their lives. And, for me, there were the skirts. I had learned so many lessons from them! Each skirt had become a "God Story" of Christ's unfailing love and His powerful work in people's lives. God used the skirts to teach me—and those who gave them as well as those who received them—many lessons of praying, listening, and responding to God. All I could say was *"The LORD has done this, and it is marvelous in our eyes."* (Psalm 118:23)

We were still talking when we heard the boarding call for our flight. We made our way on to the plane. Bob and Kathy found their two seats together, and I found my seat located further back. I sat down feeling a little lonely but knowing that I was not alone. The noise of the announcements from flight attendants and the conversations from passengers sitting around me faded into the background. Our plane taxied into position and began moving down the runway. I felt us lift into the air, and we were on our way. The lights of Nairobi slowly disappeared into the darkness. Although the continent of Africa was soon behind me, the things I learned in Africa—and all those I had met there—would be with me forever. I would never forget the sisters, the skirts, and our loving Savior who brought us all together.

If you want to pray, listen, and respond to God…
Join together with others in praying, listening,
and responding to God.

CHAPTER EIGHT - REFLECTION PAGES

"Join together with others in praying, listening, and responding to God."

PRAY AND LISTEN TO GOD AS YOU READ THESE WORDS FROM THE BIBLE

Ecclesiastes 4:9–12

Two are better than one, because they have a good return for their work: If one falls down, his friend can help him up. But pity the man who falls and has no one to help him up! Also, if two lie down together, they will keep warm. But how can one keep warm alone? Though one may be overpowered, two can defend themselves. A cord of three strands is not quickly broken.

Matthew 18:18–19

I tell you the truth, whatever you bind on earth will be bound in heaven, and whatever you loose on earth will be loosed in heaven. Again, I tell you that if two of you on earth agree about anything you ask for, it will be done for you by my Father in heaven.

1 Corinthians 12:17–21

If the whole body were an eye, where would the sense of hearing be? If the whole body were an ear, where would the sense of smell be? But in fact God has arranged the parts in the body, every one of them, just as he wanted them to be. If they were all one part, where would the body be? As it is, there are many parts, but one body. The eye cannot say to the hand, "I don't need you!" And the head cannot say to the feet, "I don't need you!"

Psalm 133:1–3

How good and pleasant it is when brothers live together in unity! It is like precious oil poured on the head, running down on Aaron's beard, down upon the collar of his robes. It is as if the dew of Hermon were falling on Mount Zion. For there the LORD bestows his blessing, even life forevermore.

Psalm 34:3–4

Glorify the LORD with me; let us exalt his name together. I sought the LORD, and he answered me; he delivered me from all my fears.

Exodus 17:10–13

So Joshua fought the Amalekites as Moses had ordered, and Moses, Aaron and Hur went to the top of the hill. As long as Moses held up his hands, the Israelites were winning, but whenever he lowered his hands, the Amalekites were winning. When Moses' hands grew tired, they took a stone and put it under him and he sat on it. Aaron and Hur held his hands up—one on one side, one of the other—so that his hands remained steady till sunset. So Joshua overcame the Amalekite army with the sword.

QUESTIONS FOR REFLECTION AND DISCUSSION

1. What blessings come from godly friendships? If you can, describe an example from your own life.

2. Because of their oneness, Donna ended up counting Nancy and Esther as one "sister" in this book. In what practical ways do you see Nancy and Esther working together in this chapter?

3. Read the story of the two widows, Naomi and Ruth, as described in Ruth 1:15–18. How does this picture of love, kindness, grace, friendship, and faithfulness encourage you?

4. Think about the stories you have read in this book. What are some examples in these stories of the Biblical truth that "two are better than one" (Ecclesiastes 4:9)?

5. Think about the seven different lessons of the seven skirt stories on how you can grow in a life of praying, listening, and responding to God. Which one of these seven lessons seems easier to you and which one is more challenging for you? In what ways would joining together with others help you work through this challenge?

6. What have you learned about God in these skirt stories that would encourage you to focus upon who He is and what He can do—no matter what your circumstances?

7. What changes are you asking the Lord to help you make in your life as a result of your time in *Seven Skirts for Seven Sisters*?

PRAYER OF RESPONSE

Lord Jesus, I praise You for being Lord of the Nations, and for Your unfailing desire to be Lord of my life. Thank you for the lessons You have taught me through these stories of the skirts. May each one of these lessons help me to grow more deeply in a life of praying, listening, and responding to You. I know that I cannot do this alone—I need your Holy Spirit, and I need others, to make this journey with me. I give my life to You—all of my challenges, my hopes, my fears, my blessings, my relationships, my past, my present, and my future. Demonstrate Your power in my weakness. Give to me the gift of a listening ear and a discerning heart. Fill me with Your courage and boldness. Move in my life in such I way that I more fully enter into, and walk in, my God-given dream and destiny. Help me to say, "Here am I! Send me! Send me!" Amen!